FIVE STEPS
FOR OVERCOMING FEAR AND SELF-DOUBT

Journey into Present- Moment Time

Wyatt Webb

HAY HOUSE, INC.
Carlsbad, California
London • Sydney • Johannesburg
Vancouver • Hong Kong

Copyright © 2004 by Wyatt Webb

Published and distributed in the United States by: Hay House, Inc., P.O. Box 5100, Carlsbad, CA 92018-5100 • *Phone:* (760) 431-7695 or (800) 654-5126 • *Fax:* (760) 431-6948 or (800) 650-5115 • www.hayhouse.com • *Published and distributed in Australia by:* Hay House Australia Pty. Ltd., 18/36 Ralph St., Alexandria NSW 2015 • *Phone:* 612-9669-4299 • *Fax:* 612-9669-4144 • www.hayhouse.com.au • *Published and distributed in the United Kingdom by:* Hay House UK, Ltd. • Unit 62, Canalot Studios • 222 Kensal Rd., London W10 5BN • *Phone:* 44-20-8962-1230 • *Fax:* 44-20-8962-1239 • www.hayhouse.co.uk • *Published and distributed in the Republic of South Africa by:* Hay House SA (Pty), Ltd., P.O. Box 990, Witkoppen 2068 • *Phone/Fax:* 2711-7012233 • orders@psdprom.co.za • *Distributed in Canada by:* Raincoast • 9050 Shaughnessy St., Vancouver, B.C. V6P 6E5 • *Phone:* (604) 323-7100 • *Fax:* (604) 323-2600

Editorial supervision: Jill Kramer • *Design:* Amy Rose Szalkiewicz

Library of Congress Cataloging-in-Publication Data

Webb, Wyatt.
 Five steps for overcoming fear and self-doubt : journey into present-moment time / Wyatt Webb.
     p. cm.
 ISBN 1-4019-0257-X 1. Fear. 2. Self-doubt. 3. Self-confidence. I. Title.
 BF575.F2W42 2004
 158.1—dc22
 2003025993

ISBN 1-4019-0257-X

07 06 05 04   5 4 3 2
1st printing, May 2004
2nd printing, June 2004

Printed in Canada

To Carin and Toby, fellow travelers. Words cannot express the joy and happiness you've brought to my life. You are truly two of the bravest souls I've ever known.

Contents

Preface **9**

Introduction **21**
   • The Five Steps to Overcoming
    Fear and Self-Doubt

Step 1:
Acknowledge the Fear and Self-Doubt **51**

Step 2:
Quantify the Fear and Self-Doubt **79**

Step 3:
Imagine the Worst-Case Scenario **97**

Step 4:
Gather Information and Support,
Confront the Perception, and
Dissipate the Fear **113**

Step 5:
Celebrate! **145**

Afterword: The Sweetness of Connection **161**
Acknowledgments **169**
About the Author **177**

❀ ❘ ❀

Preface

$\mathcal{J}$ust when I thought I'd beaten the devil, I was proven wrong once again.

For as long as I can remember, I've always wanted to get away with something, but I've never been able to do it. On November 19, 2001, I was finally convinced of the universal law of cause and effect.

For those of us who live in Tucson, Arizona, it's not often that we look outside our windows and see a puddle of water. Tucson gets about 11 inches of rain per year, most of which falls during the six-week monsoon season in July and early August. On that November day, I looked outside and noticed standing water against the retaining wall in my front yard. Upon further investigation, I discovered that somewhere underneath, inside the plumbing system, there was quite a large leak.

I called a friend of mine who does a lot of the work around my home, and he came right over. He proceeded to dig up the wet area and quickly discovered a broken pipe in obvious need of repair. On that particular day, he had a limited amount of time, so he repaired the broken pipe but had to leave before refilling the hole. I told him to go ahead; I'd take care of it myself.

I was almost finished filling in the hole and had gone around to the backyard to get the hose and wash down the sidewalk, when suddenly it felt like the biggest elephant in Africa was standing on the middle of my chest. I'd never experienced pain like that before and immediately knew it had something to do with my heart.

My wife, Carin, came outside at that moment and saw me leaning against the wall. I told her that something was very wrong. She asked me to sit down, so I did. After a few minutes, I got up and went inside the house to lie down on the bed. Nothing seemed to help, so we called 911.

When the emergency-response crew didn't get there immediately, I began to get more frightened, so we jumped into the car and headed toward urgent care, meeting the ambulance on the way. At urgent care, the staff immediately put me on a gurney, rolled me into an examining room, and upon hearing my symptoms, gave me nitroglycerin. I realized that they don't give you that for sinus problems, so my suspicions about my heart were confirmed. They worked with me for quite some time before transferring me to the emergency room at a nearby hospital.

The fear that I experienced while lying on that gurney was unlike any that I'd ever known before, and I began to look at it closely. Although I had no idea how severe my condition was, I started to feel a calmness about what was going on. I'd said for some time that I had no fear of dying, and I realized at that point that it was true. (This had been the case a great deal of my life; most of my fears have been associated with *living*.) Yet, as I looked at Carin, I became aware of how much I wanted to stay on this planet and spend more time with her. I also realized that there were things I hadn't finished doing in my work, and I wanted to complete them. Most important, I knew I'd been put in touch with my mortality. I suddenly realized that it was possible for me to leave this life at any given moment, and it became clearer than ever that I had some choices to make about how I would live my life.

❖ ⁝ ❖

He appeared
to have the soul
of a healer,
and I trusted him
immediately.

Before I go any further, let me say a few words about my doctor. I'd been assigned one cardiologist, but a man with a different name showed up. When Dr. Gregory Koshkarian put his hand on my shoulder and looked into my eyes for the first time, I just knew I was going to be all right. The sound of his voice, the way he touched my shoulder, how he treated Carin—everything he did within those first few minutes assured me that I was in excellent hands. I later found out that he was one of the premier cardiologists in Tucson and that he possessed superior technical skills, but in those first few minutes, none of that mattered. He appeared to have the soul of a healer, and I trusted him immediately.

I was admitted to the hospital and diagnosed with partial blockages in my arteries, which Dr. Koshkarian thought could be corrected with a routine angioplasty. I was scheduled to have the procedure the next day, and meanwhile I was given morphine for the pain.

After a minute or two, I asked the nurse why I wasn't getting a head rush.

He looked at Carin and asked, "Is he an addict?"

"Yes," she said, "recovering."

"Oh, that explains it," the nurse replied with a smile. Looking at me, he explained, "Mr. Webb, you don't get the rush when you use these drugs for their intended purpose, and that's to manage your pain."

Even in the midst of all the craziness, there was the opportunity to laugh.

Unfortunately, the laughter didn't last long. The next day, when Dr. Koshkarian got inside my heart, he found that the blockages were much more extensive and severe than he'd originally thought. I had 70, 80, and 90 percent blockages in five different places. He presented me with a choice: open-heart surgery or stainless-steel stents to keep my arteries open and let the blood flow. I chose the stents.

Although I was awake for the entire procedure, I had no concept of how much time went by. The whole thing was supposed to take a couple of hours, but it ended up requiring five hours and five stents. Dr. Koshkarian left the room a couple of times that I wasn't aware of and assured Carin that things were going well, proving once again that we were in the hands of the best physician and healer we could possibly be associated with. I stayed overnight in the hospital, was released the following day, and went back to work three days later.

During the first six months of my recovery time, I was hypersensitive to every little twinge that occurred. It seemed as if each little pain or skipped beat of the heart brought up fear for me. I realized that in order to deal with these particular fears (since I'd decided that I really wanted to be on this earth), I'd have to exercise what I'd been taught to do and was sharing with my clients in my work. The good news is that I had the tools at my disposal—I knew the five steps for overcoming fear and self-doubt—so once again, as I've done many times in my life, I applied them to this particular situation.

First, *I acknowledged that I was afraid* and allowed myself the luxury of being so, rather than trying to say, "There's nothing to be afraid of; you've had it fixed." Every time I experienced the fear, I addressed it, asking myself, "Why am I feeling fear?" The answers would range from, "I'm afraid the stents might not be working" to "I'm worried that something else could be wrong with my heart." I acknowledged that I'd been through a very serious procedure, and I listened when I was repeatedly told by people in the medical community and by those who'd had this procedure themselves that this was, in fact, major surgery, even though my chest hadn't been opened up.

Next, *I quantified the fear.* I asked myself, on a scale of one to ten, how much fear was present. Each time I thought my heart had skipped a beat, I felt a fear level of five or six. Then *I imagined the worst-case scenario.* At first I thought that would mean having a heart attack and dying. But when I remembered that I'd already confronted that possibility at the emergency room and realized that it hadn't bothered me so much, it helped to alleviate some of the fear. I also realized that I'd been closer to death and in more danger prior to having had the procedure than afterwards, so that helped alleviate some of it, too. Delving a little deeper, I realized that my "new" worst-case scenario was that I'd have to go through this again, and maybe next time I had chest pains they'd have to open me up. However, I knew that, more often than not, even that procedure is success-ful, so that helped alleviate the fear as well.

I then *gathered information and support to help me confront the perception and dissipate the fear.* Each time I felt threatened or felt those twinges of pain, I called Dr. Koshkarian. Being the healer that he is, he'd always call me back or have his triage nurse call to assure me that the pains had nothing to do with the possibility of a breakdown of the pro-cedure. Dr. Koshkarian and his team were avail-able to me 24 hours a day, walking me through those first six months until I was given a clean bill of health. The doctor told me that since there were no major problems, chances are that I'd be in great shape for the life that lay ahead of me. That's when it was time for the final step: *Celebrate!*

Since that time, my health has continued to improve. My arteries are flowing optimally and are as clear as they can possibly be. It's now 2004, and I'm healthier than I was 20 years ago. I don't

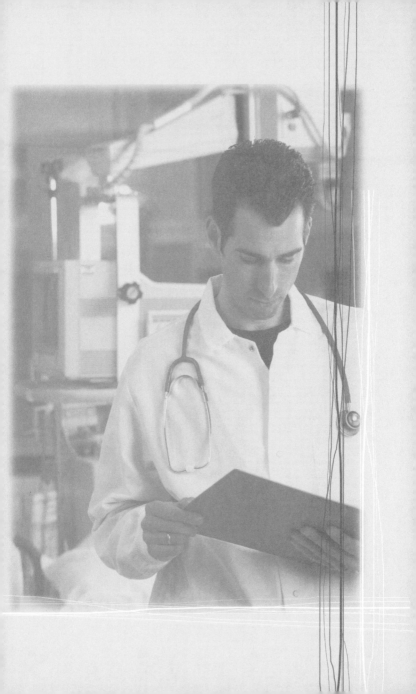

It's just a further affirmation that accountability is necessary for us to grow and remember who we are.

pay attention to every little tingle anymore; now I'm taking care of myself so as not to create future episodes of heart illness. Life is good and well worth celebrating.

So, what does all this have to do with the laws of cause and effect? Well, sometime after the procedure, my doctor told me that the blockage in my heart was probably the result of years of self-destructive living with alcohol, drugs, and cigarettes. Although I'd quit smoking cigars two years earlier and had been chemical free since 1979, my change of lifestyle had probably only postponed the inevitable. Since my cessation of drug use, I'd lived a life that I'd assumed was blessed, and in many ways it was. In truth, the laws of cause and effect hadn't let me get away with those years of abuse. They took their toll on my physical body, but the lessons I learned were invaluable.

I'm really glad to be alive and writing this book from a place of awareness that I wouldn't have had if I'd gotten away with something. It's just a further affirmation that accountability is necessary for us to grow and re-member who we are.

Introduction

*A*s I began writing this book about self-doubt and fear and the steps for overcoming them, I immediately found that I was in *need* of those steps. Feeling scared for maybe the billionth time in my life, I asked myself what qualified me to sit down and write about a subject that I obviously hadn't resolved. I suppose I had an expectation that I would've been over my fear and self-doubt now that I've entered my sixth decade on the planet, but I guess that's just another story I made up to avoid dealing with it. I'll probably never stop experiencing fear and self-doubt—I don't think anyone ever does. Maybe that's what qualifies me to write a book about the process of fear, the multitude of voices it has, and all the programming that goes into causing us humans to doubt ourselves. Maybe I'm qualified because I've constantly and successfully used the five steps in this book for confronting that programming on a message-by-message basis.

Does that mean I'll ever be totally unafraid? Probably not. Fears and doubts will always arise. As we go through the various stages and events in life, making one transition after another, we're constantly called upon to face new things that we've never confronted before. This book is not about getting rid of *all* fear and self-doubt forever and never having to face it again. Rather, this is a five-step process for overcoming fear and self-doubt whenever it arises.

Part of what I'm going to talk about in this book is my perception. I'm certainly not the final word on anything, but I do know one thing for sure: For many years of my life, I was an expert on being terrified. I did everything humanly possible to try to hide that fact, until it almost destroyed me. I can't remember when I didn't feel somewhat inferior to every other soul on the planet. That isn't the case anymore, so I'm living proof that some of these things can be healed. I'm in the process of healing even as we speak.

In my first book, *It's Not about the Horse,* I spoke about spending the first half of my life complicating everything I possibly could because I was so damn smart. At that point in time, I arrived at a place of knowing that I knew absolutely nothing. I had no answers. Upon realizing that fact, I became even more fearful than I'd ever been, but I had no map for acknowledging the fear, much less for having any idea how to deal with it, and I was extremely terrified. Only then did I realize that the answer had been there all along, and in the plainest of forms: I had to simplify my life entirely.

I'll never forget, as long as I'm on this planet, what it felt like when I was finally able to give myself permission to acknowledge to another human being that I was afraid, with no ulterior motive for saying it other than to just be honest about what was going on with me. The words were "Me, too," and they were in response to having a man whom I admired admit to me that he had awakened that particular morning feeling scared. I couldn't say "Me, too" fast enough. I was no longer dealing with something alone. I had an ally, and I wasn't the most defective person on the planet anymore. That was just a story I'd made up.

Since that time, and over the past two decades I've spent working, studying, and growing as a therapist, I've finally arrived at the five simple steps for overcoming fear and self-doubt. These days, I use the five steps to work with people all over the world in the

Melody's Story

Equine Experience, the "signature program" of Miraval Life in Balance™ (one of the world's top resorts).

Melody is a perfect example of how the five steps can get through to a person when nothing else can.

Melody's Story

Melody was a woman in her early 50s who came to my attention during her four-day stay at Miraval. When I first met her, she was at least 40 pounds overweight and walked with a pronounced limp. She was attending the Equine Experience with her sister, who had won a trip to the resort and had invited her along.

Many years earlier, Melody had had a horrible experience with horses and was terrified of them. I quickly learned that she was scared of just about everything, and had been for most of her life. Despite the fact that she'd been given opportunities to talk about her history and her childhood in general, she'd never felt safe enough to do so until this particular day at Miraval. For some reason, Melody immediately felt safe when she came down to the area where we began the session.

As we sat together with the rest of the group, for the first time in her life, Melody began to talk about being afraid. She described her first childhood memory, which occurred around the age of three and which she'd kept secret for 49 years. Until that moment, she'd been a prisoner of her own fear.

It was just beginning to snow, she remembered, when she found herself talking to her favorite teddy bear. That day, she made a serious vow to this stuffed animal that she would never hurt anyone the way her mother and sister had hurt her. Sitting under the canopy at Miraval, Melody told us that her sister was very nice now, but when their mother was alive, in order for her sister to survive, she'd sided with the mother and was a co-participant in Melody's mistreatment. Her mother was verbally abusive from day one, and Melody believed that the constant belittling, teasing, taunting, and put-downs were at the root of many of her problems.

I asked Melody what her mother had said, and she remembered hearing things like, "You're stupid, you're dirty, you should be ashamed of yourself." She went on to say that every remark that came out of her mother's mouth was an attack upon her, but that her father had loved her very much. In fact, she was seen as "Daddy's little girl," which only infuriated her mother more.

Melody believed that her mother was jealous of her relationship with her father, even though nothing unnatural went on between them. Her father was very loving, never spoke inappropriately, and certainly never touched her in an untoward fashion; but Melody believed that because he loved her so much, this incensed her mother, causing her to hate Melody in equal proportions.

As I spoke with Melody, her apparent awareness of family systems showed that she had educated herself over the years. She explained that the first child, her sister, was a girl. Melody, the second child, was also a girl. The message she received from her mother was that she was the wrong sex, that it would have been better if she'd been born a boy.

Melody told me that the verbal abuse went on into her adolescence, young adulthood, and even into her adult life, continuing until the day her mother died. She said that if she'd told her mother she'd gone to Miraval and that it was so nice and people were kind to her, her mother would instinctively say something like, "Sure they were nice. That's why it's so expensive." Anytime someone showed Melody kindness, her mother would say things like, "Of course people talk to you. They hope you come back because they want your money."

On top of all of this, when Melody was eight, she was raped by the gas man after she was left alone to wait for him to come fix the furnace. Not long after, she got her period. When her mother discovered that she was menstruating at such a young age, she called her daughter a slut.

Melody didn't tell anyone about the rape until she was almost 21 years old. And when she finally did tell her mother about it, she said, "We knew it all along. You probably asked for it."

Melody told us that she was so terrified as a child that, from age 3 all the way up to age 13, she'd often vomit in public. Her fear had taken her over physically, and literally made her sick. One day, Melody threw up in class and was made fun of by the other kids. From that point forward, she made a conscious decision that she would never throw up again. That was about 40 years ago, and she hasn't vomited since.

Melody also made a conscious decision to shut her body down so that she wouldn't feel anything. She developed the ability to separate her thought processes in such a way as to ignore the signals her body was giving her—she could even go into a trance at will. This is symptomatic of a condition known as a *dissociative disorder*, and it was just one of many sophisticated survival skills Melody had created over the years in order to avoid her emotional pain. Consequently, her life improved until she was 34, at which point she developed an infection that led to pneumonia. Running a fever of 107 degrees, Melody called both her mother and sister to let them know that she was very sick and to ask for their help.

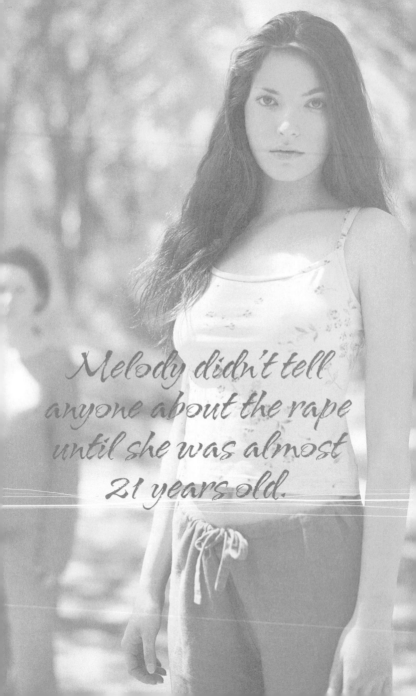

Melody didn't tell anyone about the rape until she was almost 21 years old.

Her mother's reply was, "Well, you've always been a problem to me, and now this. You're going to have to deal with it yourself."

The fever continued, and Melody began to hallucinate. She remembered being in her second-floor apartment, believing that the building was on fire and that she had to get out. Although there *was* no fire, she climbed out on the balcony and fell 35 feet to the ground, which caused her to be knocked unconscious. The next morning, she was found outside with a 108-degree temperature, and she remained in a coma for approximately three weeks.

That fall from the balcony brought about an inordinate amount of suffering that lasted for the next 17 years. Melody spent three years in a wheelchair, underwent numerous surgeries and massive amounts of rehabilitation, and eventually was able to walk again, but with a pronounced limp.

After the accident, her mother suggested that she join the Hemlock Society because they believe in physician-assisted suicide. Then, during the rehabilitation process, when Melody was sick and helpless, her mother did become a bit friendlier, but the turnaround was short-lived. Upon learning that Melody had collected a lot of money from a lawsuit, her mother once again suggested that she commit suicide so that Melody's nephew could inherit the money and go to college. Her mother thought it was unfair that her daughter had all this cash. When Melody called a suicide hotline, they said they'd never heard of a parent trying to talk their kid *into* killing themselves.

The more I heard about this woman's story, the more I understood why she presented herself as having survived more than many of us would have been physically capable of enduring. Fortunately, she'd developed several coping skills that helped her along the way. Her tremendous sense of humor was one of them: Melody said that if she hadn't been able to add humor to the telling of this story, she would have been unable to relate it and would have continued to keep it inside. In addition, she was an extremely intelligent woman, even though she described school as a washout for her. I asked how she'd become so well educated, and she replied, "Just on my own. You know, I read a lot." She also said that one of the reasons she had such a way with words was that she was always preparing for those two-against-one onslaughts from her mother and sister. "I had to learn to express myself," she explained. "I always needed a quick answer."

When I asked Melody how much fear she experienced on a daily basis on a scale of one to ten, she said it was a nine. Yet I believe that if she hadn't learned to dissociate from her feelings and find a

Until that moment, she'd always looked at herself as defective, not creative.

creative way of suppressing that fear, she truly would have succumbed. When I told her how creative she was to be able to deal with something so uncontrollable without a "toolbox" at her disposal, she was moved to tears. Until that moment, she'd always looked at herself as defective, not creative.

By the time she finished telling her story, Melody appeared to have experienced some relief. She'd looked extremely troubled when she arrived, but by the time we left the group area to walk into the arena and work with the horses, Melody seemed lighter. She was wearing a different sort of smile. It wasn't giddy or nervous, and her face seemed to be ringed in light. She'd forgotten about being thrown, and any other negative experiences she'd had around horses. For the first time in 40 years, she walked right up to a horse without hesitation. Immediately, without waiting for the usual cue, he gave her his hoof. It seemed like the most natural thing in the world, almost as if he'd looked up and seen a kindred spirit, someone just as pure as he was. As the horse did everything she asked him to do, Melody laughed with delight.

By the time we got to the round pen where participants take turns working with one horse at liberty, Melody, who'd been the most withdrawn person I'd seen in many years at the Equine Experience, was the

33

first to volunteer. She walked into the pen, looked at the horse, and smiled. Rarely have I seen anyone communicate so clearly without using their body. Normally, the horse receives its cues from the person's body language—in other words, it knows whether to walk, trot, canter, or turn and go the other way because the person indicates those commands by facing in the desired direction, turning his or her shoulders just so, and standing at the correct angle. With Melody, the horse began to trot as she laughed playfully, then he began to canter. She just stood there without using any portion of her body. I'm not exaggerating when I say this; she really didn't move. With the sheer power of her spirit, she worked the horse at three different gaits and turned him in the opposite direction, simply by being so present.

❖ ⋮ ❖

It's hard for me to put into words what I see in my heart and mind as I remember Melody in that round pen. It's almost like writing the perfect love song—words are insufficient, but I'll never forget what happened that day. It was one of the most joyful times I've ever experienced in doing my work, and it was an inspiring example of someone using the five steps to walk through fear and self-doubt.

That day at Miraval, Melody acknowledged publicly for the first time that she'd been terrified all of her life. She quantified the fear at a level of nine out of a possible ten and admitted that she'd been living that way for many years. She talked about the worst-case scenario and figured that it had already happened, so she had nothing to lose by stepping out and trying. She sure had the willingness and the guts to do just that. She had the courage to confront her old fear of horses, walk on unsteady legs up to something that weighed about 1,100 pounds, and communicate with it using the power of her spirit and a body in which she was as uncomfortable as anyone I've ever seen.

By the time we finished working with the horse and got back to the group area to process what had gone on, Melody's fellow group members were looking at her in near-awe. The smile on her lips and the glow on her face were just the beginnings of a celebration that has continued to this day. In fact, not long ago, Melody called me from her car. She said that she was looking at her reflection in the mirror, seeing herself more clearly than ever before. She knew she was different from the person she'd been for the last 50 years. She'd joined a gym and lost 40 pounds, but most important, she'd gotten tremendous relief by simply following the five-step process for dealing with the terror in her life.

Melody told me that from 1988 until she came to Miraval, she'd walked with a pronounced limp, but that was no longer the case. She said, "I think it was a combination of going to Miraval and then going home and reading your book, *It's Not about the Horse*, especially Vanessa's story."

Vanessa was a woman who'd been raped and left feeling like her body had been stolen from her. When Melody read what I'd told Vanessa—that her perpetrator or abuser didn't own her body—Melody knew that if someone like Vanessa could reclaim her body, then so could be she. So she thought, *I'm going to stop limping.*

"My life had gone down a lot further than most people's," Melody said. "It was like my body wasn't my own, but not because I was molested by the gas man. It had more to do with the suspicions and the shame of being accused of things I'd never done

The smile on her lips and the glow on her face were just the beginnings of a celebration that has continued to this day.

by my family members than with being raped by a stranger."

As she read Vanessa's story, Melody said, "I was reading the book and I couldn't put it down, but I was afraid that the material was just too heavy, and I kind of needed a breather."

She decided to go across the street to get a soda, something she normally didn't do because she never walked anywhere unless she absolutely had to. That day, she made a conscious decision to take a short stroll.

She said, "I was walking down the street, and before crossing I had to go down about a block. All of a sudden, I felt the hip joint in my left leg pop. It dropped about three-quarters of an inch and then it felt kind of sore inside. I thought, *Oh my God! This is so phenomenal!*"

After 17 years of dragging her left foot, Melody was suddenly walking normally. The synchronicity of putting one foot in front of the other was incredible for her, and it happened because she first began by *emotionally* putting one foot in front of the other.

Melody couldn't wait to share the good news with her friends, including a trainer she'd been working with at the gym. When the trainer saw how Melody was walking, she burst into tears. She couldn't believe her eyes. She'd tried so hard to help Melody with every kind of modern equipment and exercise she knew, but nothing had worked.

Melody continued, "When I went in there, it was like the glory of the coming of the Lord!" Everyone she knew was so excited for her. Her sister, her brother, and her brother's wife (a doctor) could hardly believe what had happened. Melody said, "I feel better. I look better. I'm like one of the living instead of the living dead."

I asked, "Melody, how much time do you spend during the day now being afraid?"

"Afraid?" she said, "Not much."

In just 18 months, Melody went from being 100 percent scared all the time to being unafraid 98 percent of the time. She feels as if a miracle has occured, and if this can happen, who knows what's next.

That day on the phone, she said, "I've lived very much in the past, but you know, today is wonderful. I'm on my way to Palm Springs with a friend of mine. It's a bright, beautiful day and we're in a Volvo, driving. So that's a great day, don't you think, Wyatt?" I had to agree that it was.

Melody's trip to Miraval was no accident. I think she'd been heading to a place of help for the longest time. The fact that she ended up reading a book that contained a story similar to her own just proves how important it is that we tell our stories, because they

She
feels
as if
a miracle
has occurred,
and if
this can
happen,
who
knows
what's
next.

can help others heal. Otherwise, we suffer the abuse in vain, and there's no justice. That never has been the case and won't be for as long as we're here and as long as we're willing to share our experiences.

When I talked with Melody about including her story in this book, she was delighted, but wondered why I'd want to write about someone who'd been scared 24 hours a day, seven days a week, for 50 years. I told her that it was because she's an absolute miracle!

She then told me that on the day we'd worked together at Miraval, her journey toward freedom had begun. She'd been living her life in chains, and it felt as if someone had taken them off. She felt a little sore underneath, but it was better than being shackled.

I'm so grateful to this brave woman for allowing me to use her story. The last thing I told her was something I meant with all my heart. I said, "I want you to know that meeting you has been one of the highlights of my work. I think you're absolutely delightful, and I'm grateful that you're willing to share this. Your story is going to be a huge inspiration to others, just like Vanessa's was to you."

She replied, "Oh God, I hope so. That would mean so much to me."

The Five Steps to Overcoming Fear and Self-Doubt

So, once and for all, what are these five steps I keep mentioning? Even though I touched on them briefly in the Preface, here's a handy list that you can copy and post for easy reference:

❈ *Step 1:* **Acknowledge the fear and self-doubt.** Don't minimize it, don't call it something it isn't (such as "nervousness," "apprehension," or "being somewhat anxious"). Just admit that you feel afraid or scared.

❈ *Step 2:* **Quantify the fear and self-doubt.** On a scale of one to ten, how much fear and self-doubt are you experiencing? Once you've established a level of fear, you've acknowledged just how grave you perceive the situation to be.

❈ *Step 3:* **Imagine the worst-case scenario.** What's the most horrible thing that could happen? It's important to admit to yourself, and ideally to another person, the story your mind has made up about the situation. Usually the worst-case scenario is: "I'll end up feeling humiliated and I won't be able to survive, either emotionally or physically."

✷ *Step 4:* **Gather information and support, confront the perception, and dissipate the fear.** Collect all the facts and assistance you can in regard to coping with your worst-case scenario so that it doesn't occur. Once the information and support are there, you can confront your perception. By addressing the physical situation, not only do you survive, but you're generally able to walk through the perceived difficulty. At that point, the fear automatically dissipates, you find that you're not defective, and your self-doubt disappears.

✷ *Step 5:* **Celebrate!** You've arrived in present-moment time. When you walk through your fear and self-doubt, you always end up in a place of joy.

Battling My Own Fears

Now, if this process feels like a lot of work or seems tedious, let me assure you that it isn't nearly as much work as you'll face if you postpone doing it. I remember once hearing an interview with Don Henley of the rock band the Eagles, who was asked, "How do you people, after 30 years, continue to sound as good, if not better, than you ever did?"

He said, "You have to have a tolerance for repetition."

I thought, *And in order to do that, you'd certainly have to believe in what you're repeating!* Well, let me tell you, I believe in this process. Every time it's used, I see people arrive at the place in time that's their birthright. It's a place of joy—the joy of living that's always found on the opposite side of fear and self-doubt. There's no way to go around it, under it, or over it. This process has to be gone through, but I can promise you that the rewards are well worth the effort.

Please understand that I don't see what I have to say as being "the solution" for everybody. I certainly don't have anyone's answers but my own. However, I do know firsthand that the journey itself is rewarding, and that it can spark change,

44

Celebrate!
You've
arrived
in present-
moment
time.

sometimes in the most unexpected ways. Here's an example of what I mean.

As far back as I can remember, I've carried with me a fear of heights. It's called *acrophobia,* and I'm told that a lot of people with addictive disorders also suffer from this. I certainly have it in spades. I have such a fear of heights that I have tremendous difficulty just watching a trapeze act on television. If I were to go to the top of a tall building, I'd have to stand quite a distance from the edge, and even that would feel tantamount to impending death. A 12-foot ladder frightens me; being on the roof of a normal-level house chills me to the bone.

Many years ago, I decided to fix some loose shingles on my single-story home. As I got up on the roof, I must have looked like a chicken walking on a hot stove, every step cautiously chosen. I was absolutely terrified. I had to get down and hire somebody else to fix the roof. That experience caused me to feel all kinds of self-condemnation that I never forgot. So, to document how these emotions play out in the human mind and body, I decided that, for the purposes of this book, I would attempt to overcome my acrophobia, exploring the emotions I felt during the process and utilizing the five steps I described in the last section to conquer my own fear and self-doubt.

This whole thing came about in part because of Reid Tracy, the president and CEO of Hay House, the publishing company that has put out this book (along with *It's Not about the Horse*). I was sitting in a hotel room in Scottsdale, Arizona, when Reid asked me what I'd call book number two.

As a spur-of-the-moment response, I said, *"Five Steps for Overcoming Fear and Self-Doubt."*

"Perfect," Reid replied. "When are you going to start?"

"You know, I really don't know *where* to start."

"Well," he said, "what's one of the biggest fears you've got?"

I described my acrophobia, and Reid asked me about some of the challenge activities at Miraval that have heights associated with them. I told him about the Quantum Leap, an exercise in which participants climb a 30-foot pole. When they reach the top, they step out on a little platform about the size of a pizza pan and stand up. Although they wear a safety harness, there's nothing to hold on to. For someone as terrified of heights as I am, this is no easy feat. I'd attempted it six years ago, but only got as far as eye level with the top of the pole before freezing and being unable to take the last few steps up to the platform.

Reid suggested, "Well, maybe that's where you need to start." He looked at me, laughed, and said, "So get your ass up that pole, and let's get this book done!"

As you'll see in the chapters that follow, that's exactly what I did.

"Well," he said, "what's
one of the biggest
fears you've got?"

Step 1

Acknowledge the Fear and Self-Doubt

It's almost midnight on April 16, 2003. I went to bed early tonight to get plenty of rest in preparation for tomorrow afternoon, when I'm going to do what I promised my publisher: Get my ass up that pole at Miraval. Yet I woke up approximately 30 minutes ago with my mind racing . . . and I realized that the pole isn't the problem.

I think what I'm about to confront has nothing to do with anything other than my own beliefs about myself—what I should be, *what I'm not, what others are going to see, and what I'm going to be forced to look at. The stories going through my head are endless. Sure, on a daily basis I'm able to sit with people, comfort them, and be supportive and understanding so that they might walk through their own fear and self-doubt. But now that it's my turn, it's not so easy. Intellectually, I know that I'll be strapped into the safety harness and feel physically safe as I climb the 30-foot pole. I've done that part before. However, in the past I couldn't take the last step—I didn't even try. Instead, I went through the pretense of saying, "At least I went as far as I could, and that's okay."*

Those words were nothing more than mental masturbation. Back then I had to make myself believe that it was okay. If I'd tried to take that last step, I would have had to get in touch with what I'm about to confront tomorrow. I'm not even sure what that is or what I'm dealing with right now, but I think it's about admitting the physical limitations (or the perceived physical limitations) of a 60-year-old man who hasn't taken care of his body.

I remember that as a catcher in college I was able to stay behind the plate for an entire game, bouncing up and down on my knees for nine long innings. My legs were extremely strong then, but today I feel so much pain that I can't squat at all anymore. I've lost all the cartilage between the two main bones in my legs at the knee joints. People often ask me what's wrong as they watch me walk with an unconscious favoring of whichever leg hurts the most that day.

Basically, this comes down to my fear that if people see who I really am, they'll feel sorry for me, and I'll feel ashamed. I tell people every day that it's okay to be afraid and to doubt themselves—after all, I say, we've all been programmed in this way. Well, it's not okay for me right now.

If this sounds melodramatic, it isn't—this shit is real. It's been with me forever, and I just don't want to avoid it anymore. I notice how naturally the anger comes up when I think about dealing with all this, and I'm trying to offset it. I want to be able to walk through this without raging at it. I want to work through this stuff at a deeper level than I've attempted so far. So agreeing to write this book has presented me with the opportunity to do so.

This
experience
is bringing
up the
trauma
and
beliefs
I've
carried
around
regarding
who
I
should be
as opposed
to who I
am.

If I hadn't come in here to sit down and begin to write about all this, I'm afraid I would've suffered through a sleepless night. I'm doubting myself at levels that have nothing to do with present-moment time. This experience is bringing up the trauma and beliefs I've carried around regarding who I <u>should be</u> as opposed to who I <u>am</u>. This all has to be confronted

Now I'm sure there are those who will read this and ask, "What the hell are you doing this for? Look at the things you've already overcome." Well, I haven't overcome anything 100 percent, except maybe my unwillingness to look at what's scary and to look at my shame. This shame business is really some dark stuff: It smells bad; it feels bad; it's cold and hot at the same time. But it feels like I'm close to the core of what my problems have been for much of my life.

I don't know whether I'll be able to stand up on that pole or not. I don't know if my legs will support me, and I'm going to have to deal with what's left. But at least none of this seems quite as big as it did when I woke up an hour ago.

Where Does the Fear Come From?

Step 1 in our process is to *acknowledge the fear and self-doubt*. Yet we can't do this if we don't recognize what causes us to feel afraid or insecure. So what can we do?

As you probably noticed from the above notes, one of the things I do—because I've been conditioned to respond to my fear by getting angry—is to start with my anger and trace it backwards. Finding out where fear originates or what sets it off is one way to recognize it, but we can use physical and emotional clues as well. If these clues are acknowledged early on, when we're children, then we don't have to use defense mechanisms such as anger or busying ourselves with compulsive behaviors in order to deal with our fear and self-doubt later on. We can just say, "This is what it is, and it's okay to be afraid because that's what happens to people." If we'd simply pay attention to our bodies, we wouldn't miss these clues, and we could learn to deal with fear and self-doubt in a healthy way.

Our bodies carry all of our unsolved mysteries, all of our unhealed wounds that have been covered with scar tissue. Our bodies tap us on the shoulder all the time, saying, "Hey, now's the time to deal with this." That's one of the reasons why we feel uncomfortable in our bodies, because we're constantly getting these messages that we try so hard to ignore. We've never been taught that it's okay to listen to our bodies and heal. And that's what this is all about: healing.

❖ ┆ ❖

Have you ever stopped to think about where all this fear and self-doubt comes from? Over the years, I've noticed that it all seems to originate from our cultures or our families, which are often dysfunctional in nature. The dysfunctional-family system says, "Don't talk, don't trust, don't feel." So what happens when we confront or go up against these systems in any way? Generally, we risk being labeled, and rarely is this done in a favorable way. Men who feel and show fear may be labeled as "sissies," while women who do so may be seen as "bitches" or "cold." Yet no matter what sex we are or how old we are or any other factor we can dream up, it's important to take that first step and acknowledge the fear. When it's kept secret, it's like a tumor that continues to grow: As soon as it's acknowledged, it gets exposed to the light, thus losing some of its power.

People in our culture often say things like, "You should be over that by now." But how can we be over something if we've never dealt with it? That's like telling a flat tire that it shouldn't have gone flat. Yes, it *should* have, if it had worn down to where the tread was gone and the steel showed through. The same thing can happen to us. We get all these opportunities to replace our old "tires" with new ones, and we get chances to patch or repair them, but we don't do it. If we ignore the signs long enough, we'll eventually become totally nonfunctional. It's entirely up to us to decide which outcome will occur. And that brings us to Maria.

58

Maria's Story

As I always do at the start of the Equine Experience, I sat down to talk to Maria and the six other people in her group in front of the arena where they'd soon be working with the horses. As my staff led the horses into the arena, I talked a little bit about what we'd be doing and asked each participant to tell us about him- or herself.

As Maria spoke, we all learned that this 40-something divorced mother of an 18-year-old son was absolutely exhausted. She was in constant pain, especially from her lower back up to the base of her skull. She'd been raised in Mexico City in an affluent family, but had fled that life to come to America because of the repressive culture she'd

Marisa's Story

experienced as a Mexican female. Maria had felt that women were viewed as being "less than" men, and were therefore denied the opportunities that a man would have. So when she came to this country, she believed that she'd have to do better than anyone else because of the language barrier, because she was a woman, and because she was entering "a man's world." Despite those perceived obstacles, Maria eventually worked her way up to the position of executive vice president in charge of financial development for a prominent American corporation.

When she finished her story and everyone else had taken their turn to speak, we all entered the arena with the horses. I then described the various tasks each person would have the opportunity to perform. In the Equine Experience, each participant is paired with a horse, and my staff and I show him or her how to safely approach the animal and give it a cue to raise its front hoof. The participant's job is to clean the hoof, do the same with the back leg, then brush and comb that side of the horse. Next, the person will carefully walk around the horse and repeat the process on the other side, finally untying the horse from the fence and leading it around the arena, using his or her body language to direct the animal.

As we went over the routine, Maria had more questions for me than any client I've ever worked with in a group situation. She asked about the tasks involved and possible safety concerns, but mostly she wanted to know how to "succeed." Success for her meant completing the tasks before anyone else could. She had a desperate need to win . . . and she was one of the most fear-based people I'd met in quite some time. Maria was extremely tentative with every move she made around her horse—she petted him in an exaggerated manner and spoke to him in high-pitched baby talk. This, as is quite often the case, led to the horse ignoring her and eventually going to sleep. Maria tried again to gain the horse's cooperation, but he continued to pay her no heed.

As the rest of the group continued to work, I could see that Maria was pretty much separated from any vulnerable part of herself. She was totally working in her head, and was glued to the cultural and familial wounds that she'd brought with her to this country.

I walked over to her and asked how her fear manifested itself. She talked about anger coming up for her and how she'd used it for years as a way of coping with her feelings of inadequacy and the fear of being found out for feeling such a thing. She told me that she never let anyone know she was angry;

"I never smile," she said.

it was a secret weapon for her. As I looked at her, I knew that she'd been deluding herself: Maria's ire was quite obvious. In fact, the reason I'd asked her about it in the first place was because I hadn't seen her smile once since we'd gathered with the group that morning.

"I never smile," she said.

When I asked her why, she shot back that she refused to get her needs met by flirting. Due to the treatment of females in her native Mexico, Maria had compensated by taking the warrior stance as a way of conducting her life. I encouraged her to use her anger openly—not to be aggressive toward the horse or to be critical of herself—but as a source of energy she could feed upon. I assured her that not all cultures in the world were going to be punitive toward her for using her anger as energy. I explained that she'd repressed her anger for so many years that she'd lost the choice of using it as energy and was now at its mercy when it manifested as rage.

I asked Maria to focus on herself, and she was able to do so. In doing what I asked, she began to take instruction from a powerful male and had stopped competing with me. All of a sudden, she seemed softer. She'd finally given herself permission to do something other than what she'd always done, which really wasn't working for her. When that happened, the horse began to cooperate.

63

I then questioned her about the pain she was experiencing. I asked whether she now felt a little more loose and comfortable in her body, and when she stated that she did, she smiled for the first time. She had a great smile! I acknowledged how beautiful it was and encouraged her to use it more often. Then I told her it was very clear to me that she wasn't flirting with me or anybody else, and that a smile of joy was a wonderful thing.

The group then moved on to the next exercise, in which each participant takes turns working with a single horse in the center of a 60-foot round pen. Using nothing but body language and a training whip similar to the ones used by lion tamers, I showed the group how to guide the horse around the perimeter of the pen, causing it to speed up, slow down, turn around, and stop. I demonstrated how to use the whip (it's never used to strike the animals), and position the body at various angles to communicate with the horse.

When it was Maria's turn, she kept getting ahead of the horse. She couldn't seem to stay at the correct angle to give him clear direction to go forward, so of course the horse stood still. Maria stopped in the middle of the pen and asked, "Is this horse stopping because I'm continually getting ahead of it?"

When I assured her that this was definitely the case, she announced, "Oh my God—this is how I live my life! I get ahead of myself, things don't go well, and then I'm really hard on myself."

I explained to the group that the things we learn early in life that drive us, push us, and give us physical and material success in the world are often the coping skills of children. They help create a degree of safety and reward for us, but later on they can become blocks to our happiness. Maria was able to understand this at a level that heretofore had not been possible. I told her that it was all right for her to embrace her heritage and still be a strong, assertive woman. She didn't have to cut herself off completely from her femininity and culture in order to be a successful American businesswoman.

Maria went back to working with the horse for a few minutes, and then I asked her to drop the whip, take a deep breath, and let it out. When she did, the horse immediately stopped and turned toward her. Maria started laughing—her smile had turned into laughter. I pointed out that she'd gotten to this place simply by being willing to confront a lifetime of conditioning. I couldn't help but remind her that, even though she hadn't smiled in years, she'd smiled at least eight times in the last five minutes . . . and had even started to laugh. So we began to explore the possibility of there being an endless supply of laughter and joy directly at the other end of the tenacity associated with her fear and self-doubt.

Maria looked at me and asked, "Do you really think that's possible?"

I told her that not only was it possible, it was a law.

As we sat down with the group to process the events of the day, Maria began to see how her fears and self-doubts had affected all aspects of her life. She talked about being so fearful every time her son drove her car that she required him to check in every hour to make sure that he was okay. She talked about her need for control, and how she now realized that she was actually completely powerless. She talked about having a total fear of flying, and she suddenly understood that it was actually a fear of not piloting the plane. Maria was afraid of having someone else be in charge of any part of her life, and she now knew that it was related to her history, a trauma-based familial and cultural setting of spiritual deprivation and repression.

As our time together neared its end, Maria made an agreement with the group that for the next six months she would get a massage every week. When she asked if I thought it would help, I shared an important lesson with her that had been given to me many years ago: "What do you have to lose?"

She looked at me and said, "Just some of this pain."

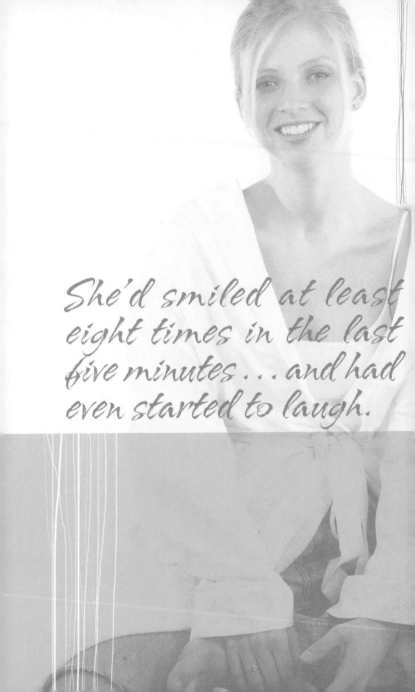

She'd smiled at least eight times in the last five minutes . . . and had even started to laugh.

Working with Maria was a joy; she was an absolute gift to me. The change that occurred on that July day in 105-degree heat was in direct relationship to her willingness to do something different to break through the protective facade she constantly carried around with her. Consequently, Maria truly arrived in present-moment time, where she received her inheritance of joy.

Being Impeccable with Our Word

Maria's story reminds me of something that happened a couple of years ago, when I was privileged to hear a speech by DON Miguel Ruiz, author of *The Four Agreements*. One of the things that struck me most about his lecture was when he talked about leaving his culture and going out into the world. His story went something like this:

> DON Miguel was raised in the Toltec tradition in Mexico, where his grandfather was a tribal elder and a shaman who was known as a great, wizened teacher. When DON Miguel left home to pursue his formal education, he rejected the teachings that he'd been subjected to in his culture. He became seduced instead by the world around him,

68

was educated as a medical doctor, and returned home with the primary intention of using his newfound knowledge to confront his grandfather's Toltec beliefs.

DON Miguel met with his grandfather, and for several hours gave him a dissertation about the primitive nature of the Toltec beliefs. When he finally finished, he looked at his grandfather and said, "So what do you think?"

His grandfather looked him straight in the eye and said, "Lies, all lies," and then proceeded to explain why. At that very moment, DON Miguel began his "graduate study" of his own culture and later became a Toltec master himself.

69

The next day, the people I work with asked if I remembered anything about the lecture. For the next hour and a half, I told them pretty much verbatim what DON Miguel Ruiz had said. I've never been able to do such a thing before or since—I certainly don't have a photographic memory—but I'd been completely open to this man who had such great power and who'd gone through a journey that had brought him to a place of truth. He was a superb communicator: He spoke broken English, but it was

He stressed
repeatedly that the most
important thing for us
to watch in regard
to our conversation
is not so much
what we say to others,
but what we say
to ourselves.

almost as if everything he said bypassed any type of filter system that was imprinted within my psyche. I was very impressed, and continue to be to this day.

One of the things that DON Miguel spoke about was being impeccable with our word. He stressed repeatedly that the most important thing for us to watch in regard to our conversation is not so much what we say to others, but what we say to *ourselves*. I'm totally convinced that this is of paramount importance, because what we tell ourselves is primarily what we'll be saying to others on a daily basis.

We absolutely must pay attention to our own stories and how we repeat them to ourselves moment to moment as we live our lives. In other words, if some of the information or programming that we've taken on doesn't work in ways that bring joy into our lives, we're obligated to change it, just like Maria did. Each of us should be a walking, breathing example of the joy of living—and the only way I know how to do that is to walk through the fear and self-doubt that we've adopted over the years as a pattern of survival. And as we do so, we change "survival" to "living." As DON Miguel says, we must be impeccable with our word: When we feel fear, we must acknowledge it; and when we feel self-doubt, we must also acknowledge it. What we say to ourselves is the most important conversation we'll have all day.

Shattering Preconceived Notions

One thing about acknowledging fear and self-doubt is that when we do, we often realize how ridiculous these emotions are. For instance, if I had a dollar for every time I've made up a story about someone in order to prepare myself for what I feared might be the inevitable, or the possibility of my getting hurt, I'd be a rich man by now. Let me tell you what I mean.

In the early 1990s, I met Judy McCaleb, whom I'd made up a story about before I even met. I knew that she was an extremely intelligent, attractive, sophisticated, and matter-of-fact woman, and I surmised that she'd risen to the top of her profession not by being the nurturing kind of female that I enjoy being around, but by being someone with a couple of steel rods down her back, or an "ice queen." I envisioned her to be a sharp, ruthless, very powerful, and self-assured woman.

Upon learning that Judy was going to be my new boss, I was immediately triggered into feeling like a helpless little boy, even though I was a middle-aged man who stood 6'4" and weighed about 220 pounds. In and of itself, my assessment of Judy as an "ice queen" was the foundation for my fear. Fortunately, I knew that if I didn't become proactive with my

72

feelings, I wouldn't enjoy coming to work the next day. So I called Judy immediately and made an appointment to meet with her the following afternoon.

When I walked into her office, Judy was sitting behind her desk in what I refer to as a "power suit," emitting enough energy to light up Delaware. Looking up at me, she asked, "What can I do for you, Wyatt?"

I said, "When I found out yesterday that you were going to be my new boss, I immediately became uncomfortable."

"Why?"

"I'm afraid of you," I replied honestly.

Her face immediately softened, but she looked puzzled as she asked, "Why is that?"

"It's not about you," I said. "It has to do with my not knowing how to deal with powerful women—it's an old thing and is among many scenarios I'm continuing to work on that scare me. This just happens to be a stopover along the way."

She smiled and said, "Well, I've been looking forward to the opportunity to work with you."

This came as a total surprise to me. Judy went on to tell me how much she admired what many people had told her about me, including my sensitivity, my kindness, and my straightforward approach to my work and how I live my life. She added, "One of the reasons I've been looking forward to working with you is that I believe you're trustworthy, because you walk your talk."

That day, thanks to acknowledging my fears and bringing them to light, I was able to begin a wonderful relationship with a truly amazing human being. We worked together for a period of months before Judy decided to resign from her position and move on to a full partnership with her husband in a successful development business here in Tucson. The day she announced her decision to leave the company was one of the most moving events I've ever witnessed. Judy was so well loved and respected that when she announced her plans to leave, half of the grown men in the room were reduced to tears.

Over the years, I've stayed in touch with Judy, who remains one of the kindest, sweetest souls I've ever met. She continues to be totally successful in her life and has shown up at Miraval on a few occasions with friends to do the Equine Experience.

I recently asked if I could write about her in this book, and she was deeply touched. Just about every time I see her, we wind up misty-eyed, remembering that day when I walked in and did my best to

That day, thanks to acknowledging my fears and bringing them to light, I was able to begin a wonderful relationship with a truly amazing human being.

clear my stuff out of the way so that I could let her into my heart. Thank you, Judy, for allowing me to use this example in these writings—but thank you most of all for being my friend.

⟡ ⟡

What has always made my life the most fertile of landscapes for spiritual and emotional growth is my willingness to acknowledge and quantify my fear, to look at the worst-case scenario, to get information that's supportive, walk through the fear, and come out on the other side with a smile on my face. Know that these steps are always available to you as well—but that *first* one is the most important. It all starts with acknowledging your fear and self-doubt. Now that you've learned how to do so, let's move on to Step 2.

⟡ ⟡

Step 2

So I'm still awake, rehearsing scenario after scenario of what might happen on that pole, and you know what? I feel embarrassed writing about this at this point in time. And as I write about feeling embarrassed, I automatically feel pissed off that I've chosen to climb a 30-foot pole later today.

Since I already know that I'm afraid, I've begun to quantify the fear, which from moment to moment varies. It goes all the way from doubting myself emotionally and spiritually to questioning my own worth as a human being—certainly my worth as a man. If you ask me to tell you how much fear and self-doubt I'm experiencing on a scale of *one to ten, sometimes it's <u>beyond</u> a ten. Mostly, though, it's probably in the area between five and eight, because my head takes over and rationalizes at times.*

I'm going back to bed now so that I might sleep, so that maybe my challenge won't be more difficult than it needs to be because I didn't get enough rest. Life is zoo-y sometimes!

What's in a Name?

For many of us, particularly men, acknowledging fear and self-doubt isn't always easy because we've been taught in our culture to minimize everything we feel. We've grown up watching football players on the field who take a brutal hit and then slowly get back on their feet and say, "No big deal." We've heard our parents tell us, "Don't be such a baby. Big boys don't cry."

In order for men to acknowledge fear, we quite often have to be at the point of getting ready to do battle, tear something up, scream, or throw something, when in fact we've been angry for days prior to that. Most men don't even want to use the word *anger*, let alone the word *fear*. We'd rather call it "being a little frustrated" or "feeling a little irritated."

It doesn't make any sense to me that we have eight or ten words to describe one emotion. If we picked up a key to a car and someone asked what it was, we'd say, "It's a key." But if we employed the same system to describe a key that we use to describe our emotions, we might call it "an opening device," "an entry-level instrument," "an igniting tool"—anything but what it really is. It's a friggin' key!

Listen, fear is fear, anger is anger, and shame is shame. If we're going to identify how much fear we have, let's start by calling it what it is. Let's not say, "I'm a little nervous" or "I'm feeling some trepidation." Let's just admit, "I'm scared, all right! *I'm scared.*"

As I said, for many men, this can be a very difficult concept—but for Jack, it was almost impossible.

Jack's Story

When I first met Jack, he was a 64-year-old recovering alcoholic who had been clean and sober for 12 years. He told me that he'd transitioned from chemical addiction and alcoholism to workaholism, which ultimately made him an extremely wealthy man. He also claimed that his job was his identity, and that he'd been an overachiever since the age of nine. Yet despite his considerable career triumphs, he'd been in deep physical pain and suffered from

Jack's Story

severe bouts of depression. It seemed to me that this man had few coping skills for handling his fear and pain. So, since he said he'd felt "a deep connection" to me and sensed that I could help him with his ailments, I suggested that he come to a three-and-a-half-day intensive workshop I facilitated at Miraval.

During our first day of experiential work at the Equine Experience, Jack was a physical and emotional wreck. As one of the women in the group worked with her horse, she asked Jack to come into the arena to be of emotional support to her. He was sitting on a crate, and he was so shaky that two people had to help him up. His body was so saturated with fear that it was taking away the power of his muscles and skeletal system. It was one of the deepest manifestations of fear invading a person's body and robbing first his spirit and then his physical being that I'd ever encountered in my entire career.

On the second day of the workshop, Jack told me, "I totally need to work this afternoon. I'm terrified and feeling helpless."

I asked him to step into the center of the room we were meeting in and sit down on a throw pillow that I'd placed on the floor. I joined him there and asked him to tell the entire group his life story so that we could attempt to support him in easing his pain.

It wasn't easy for Jack to open up to us, but he finally admitted that his father was an alcoholic, and his parents divorced when he was five years old. The next year, his mother committed suicide, and Jack was the one who found her. Until he was 52 years old and went into recovery, Jack had been unwilling to acknowledge his mother's suicide. Instead, he'd completely repressed the cause of her death with chemicals and work for all those years.

After his mother's death, Jack's father signed his son's custody over to his own parents, a scenario that turned out to be disastrous. Jack's grandparents abused him physically and verbally for years. And when he was only nine years old, his grandmother told him that his father had given him away with the understanding that he would never take him back. She also said that Jack would never amount to anything because he was his father's son.

Jack then went on to tell us about his five marriages. Even though he was happy with his present wife and they had entered into recovery together, he still vividly recalled his second and third wives telling him the same thing that his grandmother had: that he'd never amount to anything. Each time he heard those words, he'd sucked up a big breath inside and thought, *God dammit, I will, too! You'll see!* Given his rage, and his drive to prove them all wrong, he went on to become a very rich man.

As he spoke, I observed that Jack appeared to be in a childlike state. When I asked him how old he felt, he immediately went to nine years of age. When I then asked him to quantify his fear on a scale of one to ten, he told me he was about an eight. It didn't take long to discover that Jack had been stuck in a nine-year-old traumatized emotional state for most of his adult life, with an extremely high amount of fear and self-doubt stemming from his experiences. And even though Jack had gone through four marriages in an adult man's body, he'd done it with the emotional coping skills of a very terrified, insecure little boy. When I asked him if this assessment seemed accurate, he immediately agreed that he'd never known how to be a husband; in fact, deep down inside he felt that he had no idea what he was doing most of the time.

Jack's task was to work on separating the traumatized child from the man sitting on the cushion on the floor. That day, we created a safe setting for his own spiritual awareness in order to create a safe place internally. With his eyes closed, Jack used his breath to bring himself into present-moment time, without losing sight of the wounded and devastated nine-year-old boy. As a result, he was finally able to become the parent he'd never had—a healthy, nurturing, understanding caretaker. He could then relieve the little boy of being responsible for anything other than being taken care of by the soon-to-be-retired adult. Jack acknowledged and quantified the pain that this child had gone through all his life and was finally able to say, "I now know what to do with my retirement years—I'm going to become the parent to myself that I never experienced."

As Jack concluded his work, I looked around the room to see that everyone was in tears, expressing huge amounts of compassion toward him as he sat there on the floor. I also noticed that Jack's face had grown softer and his brow was not nearly as furrowed. Even though he was clearly quite emotional, he was also visibly calmer and more at peace.

I knew intuitively what was about to happen next. (Keep in mind that during the previous morning's work, Jack had needed assistance to get up and walk into the arena to help a fellow participant.) I told him, "What I'd like you to do now is stand up," and Jack sprang to his feet! There was a gasp from the entire room, accompanied by cheers and applause. Jack looked totally surprised, and his tears were replaced by a beaming smile. It was a moment of total elation for us all.

Throughout the remainder of the workshop, Jack would spontaneously say, "I need a moment!" Then he'd jump up and throw his hands up like a circus performer. This was such a manifestation of the spiritual power of a man who'd given meaning

This was such a manifestation of the spiritual power of a man who'd given meaning to his pain.

to his pain. And in the process, he was able to discover the self-worth that he hadn't known he'd possessed all along.

I spoke with Jack several weeks later, and his condition was still improving. What a gift he was to myself and the 26 other people in the group over those three days.

Warning: Overload!

Situations like the one that happened with Jack make me feel grateful to be on this earth. It was wonderful and gratifying to watch him walk through absolute terror and come out on the other side, where he learned that there was nothing wrong with him as a human being and his fear was no longer in charge of his life. It also gave me the opportunity to witness the miracle of the human spirit, and to realize that acknowledging our fears is the first step in making miracles happen.

Yet after we've acknowledged the fear for what it is, we're then forced to take the next step and ask ourselves, "How much is there in my body?" As you may have noticed, when it comes to quantifying fear, I recommend giving it a number from one to ten.

Now, if we've been trained to be self-critical, we won't want to acknowledge that we're feeling a seven or an eight. Oh my God, what would people think? That we're wimps, we have no social skills, and we shouldn't be in the position we're in? That we shouldn't have lived this long and don't deserve to be here? That we've fooled them so far, but when they find out, they'll fire us or divorce us?

Chances are they'd think, *I understand that!* You see, all those things that we're sure other people will think are just stories we've made up in our heads. And remember from the last chapter how ridiculous those stories can get!

It's so imperative to quantify the fear. When you simply admit, "This much is present," it makes it seem manageable. When it's not as big as Mt. Kilimanjaro, you can hold it in your hands and deal with it. However, it's equally important not to overestimate these emotions or give them more power than they deserve. If you're feeling a fear level of ten, it means that you believe you may not survive. But just because it *feels* like a life-threatening ten doesn't mean your life is really in danger.

In other words, unless you can look in front of you and see a man-eating predator or someone holding a gun to your head, chances are that what you're calling a ten is not about what's going on right now. It simply means that what you're presently facing reminds you of, or is bringing up, something

that you haven't dealt with, something that trauma-tized you earlier in life.

If you could take one big breath and ask, "Is there a man-eating tiger in front of me? Or is some-one holding a gun on me?" you'd realize that you were simply on overload. Your fear is out of propor-tion to the current event. It's much like cranking up the volume on a sound system: In a high-quality system, the speakers can handle it; with an inferior system, the speakers will blow out.

Giving yourself a reality check by asking ques-tions about what's really going on will help you step out of the fear and into present-moment time. Skip this step and you'll find yourself experiencing an anxiety attack, hyperventilating, or breathing into a brown paper bag . . . and often seeing yourself as defective for feeling that way.

How many times in your life have you thought, *I may not make it through this?* Well, you *did* made it through! The proof is that you're here, reading this book. The only reason you're feeling the fear again is because you haven't dealt with it yet. Overload is simply your body's way of trying to tell you, "You've held this in for a long time. Listen up, you're not going to die here—you've just been given a chance to deal with this thing." In fact, a lot of times, a fear level of ten is just a huge opportunity for your spirit to say, "It's time to heal this. You've postponed this long enough, so it's time to enhance the quality of your life. Get this out of the way so that the flames don't burn up everything in sight."

You don't have to feel this way over and over again. All it takes to end the cycle is your willingness to address the situation. Every day, you wake up with the ability to ask yourself, "How do I want life to be today? And what am I going to do about it?" Willingness interrupts the cycle and lets you heal. Life will still go around and come around, but just like that tire I mentioned in Step 1, it doesn't have to go flat this time. It can roll along more smoothly when you quantify the fear and take the steps toward healing.

Another Chance to Learn

Sometimes when a problem seems insurmountable and we think it's a seven, eight, nine, or ten, our fear keeps us immobilized, and we won't even take the first step toward overcoming it. This happens to all of us, again and again, but the more we practice, the easier it becomes.

As I began working on this book, I found myself stuck. I'd gotten about a third of it written, but then I didn't know what to do or say next. I started thinking, *I've already taken the money and used it. I'll need to pay the publisher back because I don't know*

*if I can deliver this book. How the hell am I going to
do this?*

In the midst of all this, my wife commented that
I seemed troubled. I admitted, "I'm afraid that I can't
do this."

She asked, "How afraid are you?"

"It's about a nine or a ten, or maybe even worse.
I'm afraid I'm just a one-story guy, and I really don't
have anything else to say," I answered.

"Okay," Carin said. "Now you know what you're
dealing with."

She was right—now I knew what I had to do.
And then I sat around kicking myself in the ass,
wondering how many more times the universe was
going to show me how to get past situations where
I feel inferior or afraid. I still don't know the answer
to that question, but I do know that I began to trust
the process a little more. I have to add that the tim-
ing was amazing: It certainly seems like universal
perfection that I got mired in my own stuff and had
to use the steps just when I was writing about them.

Because of my own fear and self-doubt, I hadn't
used the resources that were so readily available to
me. All I had to do was have a little faith, confront
the story I'd made up, and take that first step on the
hero's journey. No matter what path in life we're on—
whether we want to write a book, swim across a
river, climb a mountain, jump out of an airplane, or

No matter what path in life we're on—whether we want to write a book, swim across a river, climb a mountain, jump out of an airplane, or climb a 30-foot pole—chances are we'll have the opportunity to fight our own misperceptions about how capable we are.

climb a 30-foot pole—chances are we'll have the opportunity to fight our own misperceptions about how capable we are. If we're willing to do that, we'll complete the hero's journey every day, in every act in which we participate. Every time we confront our misperceptions, we'll come up with a pearl. We may expect to find something funky, but we'll usually discover a prize. It doesn't happen by chance, though; it happens by participation. We have to be willing to take those first few steps. So let's get to Step 3!

Step 3

Imagine the Worst-Case Scenario

My wife, Carin, has agreed to be with me to support me later today, as well as to tape my climbing the pole so that I might be able to look at it in a different light after the fact. One of the reasons I'm doing this is so that I can present to you, the reader, the dynamics of how fear has played a part in my life all these years, even after I gave up the drugs and alcohol that repressed my feelings. Almost 24 years after becoming sober, I'm continuing to deal with what I'd put off for the first 36 years of my life: fear in all of its manifestations, self-doubt, and the shame of what it has meant for me to be a human being.

I'm really afraid for anybody to see what I've got left after all these years—hell, I'm afraid of what I've got left! I know that Carin is supportive, but I don't want her to see who she's really married to. She's younger than I am by about 19 years, and my fear is that she'll see me as an old man. That's my story, I know, certainly not hers. I don't really know what her story is . . . I've been too busy criticizing myself to get an update from her.

I look at Hollywood types who are around my age, like Harrison Ford, and I know that being 60 or 70 is not a death sentence. After all, when Clint Eastwood was in his early 60s, he certainly wasn't a man to be dealt with lightly. Of course I probably couldn't be the pace car in a foot race for 40-year-olds, but that's not what I'm dealing with right now.

If I don't go to the top of that pole, my worst fear is that I'll be seen as incompetent, which is even worse than being a coward. The other thing that could happen is that I may get to the top and stand up on that thing and suddenly have no faith in the fact that the rope is going to hold me.

I guess I'll have to deal with this in layers, just like peeling an onion. Every time you peel back one layer of that vegetable, there's more onion there, more to uncover. The closer we get to the core, the more profuse our tears, because we've been at it for so long. It's similar to the old axiom, "The closer to the gate, the fiercer the lions." That saying really is true.

Just My Imagination . . .

The third step in overcoming fear and self-doubt is easier than it may sound: To imagine the worst-case scenario simply means thinking of the most horrible thing that could possibly happen, then bring it into consciousness and see how much of it is based in reality. These scenarios often involve statements such as, "People will dislike me," "They'll think I'm stupid," "I won't survive this," or "I'll be perceived as being faulty or weak." These fears are usually based on how we feel about ourselves, not on how someone else feels about us. We're just externalizing our own emotions.

Have you ever noticed what tends to happen when we admit our worst fears to another person? They usually respond with, "I have no idea what you're talking about. Where did you ever get that idea?" I've had that happen more times than I can

Worst-case scenarios tend to be nothing more than stories.

count. In other words, worst-case scenarios tend to be nothing more than stories.

We can prove this to ourselves by looking back at some of the worst things we've imagined in the past and seeing whether or not they came true. Chances are, they never manifested at all. I'd guess that 98 percent of the stories we make up in our heads have no validity or possibility of happening—the odds against them ever coming true are greater than any in Las Vegas.

There are exceptions, of course. Sometimes our worst fears *do* come true through the laws of the universe, but that's usually a result of keeping them secret. If we want to make sure that these horrible scenarios actually occur, all we have to do is keep them to ourselves, and they will. But if we bring them into consciousness, they probably won't. The choice is ours—after all, we don't *have* to heal. I don't think the deity will get mad at us if we don't. We'll just end up uncomfortable, because the solution is always at hand.

Sometimes our worst-case scenarios also come true because they're based on physical illnesses that can't be stopped. We still have some incurable diseases on this planet—things like pancreatic cancer and liver cancer are pretty deadly, and few people survive them. But even if our worst-case scenario is, "I'm afraid that this person is going to die," and it's likely to come true, we still have some choices. We can choose to spend the remaining hours, days, and months being preoccupied with our fear, or we can accept the fact that this type of illness usually causes death, and choose to spend quality time with our loved one. Rather than focusing on the disease, we can decide to spend our time talking about how much we care about the person, making sure that they hear what we have to say.

Is any of that comfortable? No, because we've never been taught on a deep enough level that it's impossible for us to die. We've been taught to believe that if someone leaves, they take away something we can never have again. I think that a lot of the pain we experience around loss is the belief that happiness has to do with an outside source— be it a person, a pet, or a treasured possession. Maybe we've set up ways to feel this pain. Maybe we make it harder than we need to because of our own fear and self-doubt. I say "maybe" because I don't know. Let's ask ourselves this question: Do we make life harder than we need to because of our own fear and self-doubt? I think that for me, the answer is probably yes.

This next story shows how empowering it can be to imagine and confront our worst-case scenarios as the next step in overcoming fear and self-doubt.

Veronica's Story

Veronica came to one of my three-day programs not long ago. As we started our first group
session, she explained that she was in the midst of
going through a divorce. Her 12-year marriage had
produced four children whom she loved deeply,
but she described the experience as "sleeping with
the bogeyman," since her husband was verbally
abusive and constantly degraded her.

Veronica said that the abuse had increased
gradually over time. She tolerated it in the beginning,
blaming it on her husband's upbringing in an
extremely rigid, male-dominated Midwestern farm-
ing family. After the first two years or so, she'd
begun to believe the things he said about her, which
caused her to feel less capable and worthy as a
person. But that was only one of her reasons for
staying in the marriage. Since Veronica and her
husband had become quite successful as farmers,
developing a considerable amount of wealth and all
the trappings that came with it, she'd come to believe
that the money itself was a good enough reason to
stay in the abusive relationship.

For a while, Veronica distracted herself by
designing her own home, throwing herself into the
details of how it would look both inside and out. In

obsessing over the house, she tried to deal with her internal pain by using an external route. But when her husband threatened to harm the children, she left the marriage immediately.

As I listened to her speak, it became obvious to me that one of the ways Veronica had dealt with her past was to intellectualize, to go as far up into her head as she could—and she'd brought a lot of rage back with her. When she told us, "I'm going to raise these children by myself. I know I can, and that's all there is to it," there was a huge amount of energy attached to her words. When I asked her to assess how much pain was at the foundation of all the anger she was repressing, she immediately retorted, "I've dealt with this! I'm ready to move on and am happy with my life now."

I asked Veronica whether her husband had been the first male who'd ever spoken to her in a degrading manner. She lowered her eyes immediately, her lip began to quiver, and she squeaked out, "No." She admitted that she'd been treated this way by her father and older siblings, and for the most part she'd been seen as a second-class citizen because she was female. It was no accident that Veronica and her husband had found each other—after all, they were pulled together like magnets to bring up those things that needed healing.

As we looked a little closer, Veronica began to see that she hadn't gotten through the pain of her marriage. When I asked her why she was so adamant about having worked through it and why she took such an angry stance, she admitted, "I'm just terribly afraid to feel this."

I asked her if she'd be willing to participate in the steps for overcoming fear and self-doubt, but she swore at the prospect, saying, "Dammit to hell, I thought I'd already done it."

Quite often, we deal with these types of things in stages, especially if we try to do it without any guidance. We may acknowledge the presence of the fear or the pain, but then we intellectualize it, wrap it up in a nice package, and storing it away with a modicum of relief, believing that we've dealt with it. In truth, we've only *repressed* it, putting it away until such time that we might feel safe in taking it out again.

I suggested to Veronica that the time was now—she was out of the marriage and no longer felt threatened by this man, and she'd walked away with a certain amount of financial independence and a belief that she could raise her children alone in a better fashion than she could with her husband. So since she'd already acknowledged her fear and self-doubt, I asked her to take Step 2 and quantify how much fear she was experiencing. When she told me it was a nine out of a possible ten, in spite of her relief at being out of the marriage, I asked her where she thought all that fear was coming from.

She replied, "I don't have any idea. I really don't have that much to fear now."

"Well," I continued, moving on to the next step, "what's the worst possible thing that could happen?"

She thought for a moment and said, "I could repeat this relationship. After what I've just learned, it looks like I re-created my original family in the marriage. I'm terrified that I might do it again and create danger for both myself and my kids."

I then asked her how deep she was willing to go to work with me on this. When she indicated that she was ready to do whatever it took, I delved a little further. I asked her how old she felt, as her fear was obviously being driven from a trauma place. When she softly answered, "Twelve years old," I asked her to close her eyes and get an internal picture of her young self. I encouraged her to access the memory of how it felt to be a terrified little girl in a dominant family culture that hadn't valued females as much as it did males.

Veronica told me that she'd felt so alone, and she desperately needed someone to understand. As we continued to work, she was able to take the wounded, 12-year-old part of herself and bring that little girl into present-moment time, to the place

in Arizona where we were working together that day. We developed a plan for the frightened child by teaching her to listen closely, parent her, create safety for her, and make a commitment to never take her into another abusive situation. By this time, Veronica had stepped out of that 12-year-old place—where she was certainly not capable of being a mother, a wife, or someone who had any idea of how to create safety—and had given direction of her life to a present-day, 30-year-old adult.

At the conclusion of her work, after which her fellow group members gave their impressions of what they'd seen and heard, Veronica looked me directly in the eye and said, "I need to tell you something, Wyatt. I feel like a woman for the first time in my life." She was smiling and crying all at the same time—it was a total celebration.

I congratulated Veronica for finally acknowledging the pain, the fear, and the self-doubt she'd quantified as a nine out of a possible ten. Realizing that she'd been operating out of a truly traumatized state, she was finally able to confront her worst-case scenario and transcend it.

I went on to work with Veronica for two more days in the group process. She continued to celebrate her womanhood and to feel the power of what that truly meant. When she found herself being triggered again as other levels of the fear or the abusive past came into play, she utilized her newfound skills, imagined the worst-case scenario, and asked herself, "What is this going to be like days, or even months, from now?" She'd learned how to use the five steps to bring herself back into present-moment time and create that place of safety that always exists in the here-and-now.

These were important breakthroughs for Veronica, and it was a joy and privilege to observe the process.

She'd learned how to use the five steps to bring herself back into present-moment time and create that place of safety that always exists in the here-and-now.

Step 4

Gather Information and Support, Confront the Perception, and Dissipate the Fear

It was time. I showed up at the Quantum Leap and was greeted by Joe and Kevin, both of whom are Miraval employees and expert facilitators for this event, and they helped prepare me for my climb. And, of course, Carin was there with camcorder in hand.

Last night, I'd run through the first three steps in this process of overcoming fear and self-doubt. Now it was time to take the next step—gather information and support. I talked to Joe about what I perceived to be my physical limitations, letting him know that I often defend myself against being afraid by becoming sarcastic or using anger as a defense. I then asked him and Kevin to call me on it if they saw me doing that. After they agreed, I proceeded to get into the harnesses, helmet, and all the equipment necessary for climbing the 30-foot pole. I was ready.

There's No Shame in Asking

I'll bet that if I asked any group of people, "What does our culture say about people who ask for help?" nearly every one of them would answer, "That they're weak." Now if asking for help means we're weak, then in order to be strong we'd have to know everything, which is impossible. No, in order to make it through the fear and self-doubt, we're going to need some assistance.

I find it interesting that we seem to be willing to ask for help in some areas of our lives, but not all. That is, we'll use the Internet to look things up, or we'll go to a doctor with questions about our physical health, and we may even ask for a second or third opinion in some instances. But rarely will we even ask for a first opinion about our spiritual and emotional lives.

Why do we do this? Basically, it comes down to our stories again, which are usually in the vein of "People will think I'm stupid, weak, and flawed." In other words, we tell ourselves that we have to be perfect in everything we do. Intellectually, we know better than that, but on a cellular level, we've bought into the idea that we can never show "weakness." Well, we've got to let go of this fairy-tale perspective, acknowledge that it's all right to have limitations, and simply ask for help when we need it.

One of the things that keeps us stuck in our fear is failing to ask for help because we talk ourselves out of it. We worry, "What if nobody understands? What if they don't care enough? What if they don't have what I need?" The answer is simple: If that happens, we just need to ask somebody else. Gathering information means that we just keep asking until we find someone who can answer. Although we may get rejected a few times in the beginning, with more practice and experience, we'll soon get a feel for who can help and who can't, or who will and who won't. And as we become more willing to step out, our intuition gets honed more and more.

At the risk of sounding sexist, I suggest that if you're a man and you want to know more about developing your intuition, you should ask a woman. After all, in our culture, women have had permission to trust their hunches forever, and they might be able to help you develop yours. You might say, "What is this intuition thing that you have? How does that work? Can you help?"

What would it mean in this culture for a man to ask a woman for help? If you're thinking, *In a patriarchal culture, it would probably be a shameful thing,* then that's just a story that you've made up in your head. Stories like those are the major impediment to peace, happiness, joy, and love. They keep us isolated and afraid, and they permit our self-loathing. They're nothing more than a kind of conditioning, a way of programming that's become obsolete. It's time to erase the computer, set up a different password, and reprogram the whole damn thing. You could even call the new program THERE'S NO SHAME IN ASKING, VERSION 2.0.

When we gather information and support, we take the next giant step toward overcoming fear and self-doubt. Armed with the facts, we're then ready to confront our fears and walk through them to present-moment time. That's just what Cliff did.

Cliff's Story

Before I begin, I'd like to insert a brief disclaimer. I grew up in the southeastern United States, and one of the things that's really prevalent there are stories about taboo subjects like bodily functions. They're seen as being really funny, probably because talking about them brings relief from some pretty

Cindy's Story

repressive cultural beliefs. In my 60 years on this earth, I haven't lost my enjoyment for these kinds of stories. When my friend Cliff told me this one, I lost my breath halfway through from laughing so hard. I just had to include it in this book in order to lighten up the serious tone I've got going here so far. I hope it doesn't offend anyone. If it does, maybe another misperception needs to be confronted!

It seems that Cliff had gone to downtown Tucson with his dog in his truck. If you travel on these streets, you'll see that quite often—a man with his dog (or dogs) in a truck. Sadly, because of our high temperatures, there have been repeated cases of dogs suffocating in the heat, so the city passed an ordinance making it illegal to leave an animal in a parked vehicle, regardless of the time of year.

On this particular day, that ordinance became significant to Cliff. He and his dog were traveling along when they got stuck in traffic. Being pressed for time, Cliff became increasingly frustrated and began to feel somewhat anxious. For most people, this wouldn't be a big deal, but Cliff has suffered from an anxiety disorder for a great deal of his life. When he experiences the onset of an attack, he tends to develop sudden gastrointestinal distress. In other words, Cliff was stuck on the streets of downtown Tucson with an immediate urge to go to the bathroom.

Remembering the dog ordinance, his anxiety only grew. He worried, *I can't park the truck and run into a service station or any other establishment and ask to use the restroom, because it would cost me $750 to $1,000 if I left my dog in the truck!*

Weighing the alternatives in his mind, Cliff knew he had an immediate dilemma: *I just got this truck, so if I poop in it, I'm going to ruin it. I can't jump out and park on the side of the road because I'm in a residential neighborhood, and there isn't enough vegetation in the desert to hide me. I'm in deep trouble!*

At that point, Cliff remembered the steps for overcoming fear and self-doubt. Trying to be calm, he quickly ran through the first three steps. He asked himself, *Am I afraid? Of course I am! I'm having an anxiety attack. On a scale of 1 to 10, I'm feeling about a 10 or 11. What's the worst thing that can happen? I can shit my pants and ruin my truck!*

Then he remembered Step 4: Gather information to avoid the worst-case scenario. Cliff suddenly remembered that he not only had the dog in the truck, he also had some disposable bags for cleaning up when he took the dog to the park. That's when he realized: *My windows are tinted . . . I could just use one of those doggie bags!*

As soon as Cliff had information, his anxiety subsided. He knew he had choices, which meant that the fear was not in charge of what would happen.

*Gathering
information
doesn't
always
mean
talking to
someone else—
sometimes the
resources
we need
are right
inside of us.*

His sense of urgency diminished, giving him immediate relief from the need to relieve himself in his
truck. Because the fear dissipated, he was able to
make it home in time (although he did say that he
ran without stopping from his truck to the bathroom). His truck was intact, so was his laundry, and
so was his fear quotient. He was able to overcome
fear and self-doubt in an everyday circumstance
that I'm sure many of us can identify with. He also
showed that gathering information doesn't always
mean talking to someone else—sometimes the
resources we need are right inside of us. That was
an important lesson for me to learn as I faced going
up that pole.

121

Conquering the Pole

After Kevin and Joe helped me get into my harnesses and helmet and check the equipment, I began
my climb up the 30-foot pole. Now, when I say
"pole," that's exactly what I mean. Picture a big telephone pole in the middle of nowhere. Attached to
the side is an aluminum ladder that goes about ten
feet up from the ground. After that, pairs of huge
staples are driven in side by side—and they're just
large enough to use as handholds and to stand on
with your feet.

As I began climbing up the ladder, I felt as if my feet weighed somewhere between 30 and 50 pounds apiece. On the plus side, I quickly realized that all my worries about whether my shoulders or knees would fail were just stories I'd made up. During the entire climb, I didn't feel one twinge of pain from any of my joints. This might have been due to the adrenaline flowing through my body, but whatever the reason, I didn't feel any physical pain. None. All the pain was purely emotional.

When I reached the top of the ladder and no longer had side rails to hold on to, all of a sudden the dynamics changed. One of my supports was gone (as is sometimes the case in life), so I had to reach up and grab on to the staples, which had nothing on either side of them. As I worked my way up one hand at a time, one staple after another, each move became more terrifying than the last.

I realized that my breath had become labored, not from physical exertion, but from fear. Since I knew that my body needed oxygen desperately, I began to take a few deep breaths. Then I started getting angry, which as I've mentioned before is my normal mode of operation—get scared, get embarrassed, get mad. With the ladder far below and nothing to support me but those large staples, I felt my legs quiver a little, and I heard myself say aloud, "I fucking hate this." This immediately gave me energy and stopped my legs from trembling, so I said it again louder: "I fucking hate this!"

I stopped, breathed deeply for a minute, and then continued my ascent. I was getting encouragement from Kevin and Joe on the ground, but I was pretty much ignoring them. (I can't even remember what they were saying.) When my head reached the top of the pole, and the platform was just above eye level, I realized that I'd made it to the same level that I had six years ago, when I'd decided not to go all the way. All of a sudden, my fear level escalated beyond a ten, and my body froze. Standing on those large staples, I felt as if the harness didn't exist. Fear had temporarily taken over my entire system. As a grown man, I'd never felt as powerless or as helpless as I did in that moment.

I said, "I'm frozen."

Joe and Kevin encouraged me to breathe, which I did. Then they called up to me, "Just try to take one more step."

Shakily, I replied, "I don't think I can."

They encouraged me to be still for a moment and then take another step, which I was able to do. My head still hadn't cleared the platform area, because my knees were bent. (And I still had absolutely no joint pain. Incredible.) Suddenly, I knew that I had the physical strength to do this. I stood up straight and my head cleared the top of the platform; in fact, it was almost at chest level. I'd gone beyond what I'd done before!

This time, I knew that I had to get on top of that pole, but I was absolutely terrified to do so. That little platform is really tiny once you get up there—about the diameter of a medium-sized pizza pan—and I didn't think it was possible for me to stand up on it. That's when I said, "I'm going to try to sit down on this damn thing." I knew I had to put my body up there somehow. If I couldn't stand, I could at least sit. That would constitute a victory for me.

Kevin and Joe called up, "Well, maybe you want to think about possibly—"

"That's it!" I yelled out, gesturing impatiently with one hand. "This is as far as I need to take this."

"Okay," they replied.

I managed to pull myself up on top of the pole, sit down, and look around. I wasn't feeling elated, victorious, or satisfied. Mostly, I just felt afraid, alone, and sad.

I called down to Joe and Kevin and told them that I'd had enough. I asked them to catch me because I was jumping off. Sliding one foot around behind me, I put my hands on the platform, took a step down, and let go. I fell into the safety of the harness, and they carefully lowered me down.

When I got to the ground, there were congratulations all around, but I couldn't really take in any

Mostly,
I just
felt afraid,
alone, and sad.

of it. I realized how lonely I was, how once again no one else's perception of what I'd done or how successful I'd been really mattered to me. I'd been alone in this respect all my life. Something needed to come from within to fill this lonely hole, and I wasn't aware of what that was.

After getting out of the harnesses, I sat down with Carin, Joe, and Kevin and began to process what had happened. Carin talked about some of the behavioral aspects of my personality that had manifested themselves on top of the pole that day. She observed that it was quite typical of me to make a definitive statement when I had my mind made up, and because of the personal power that I'm perceived to possess, no one ever questions me or pushes me to go any further. I not only set boundaries, I generally set them with a vengeance, and people rarely attempt to cross them.

Carin also thought I was quite ingenious to figure out a way to be on top of the pole without standing up on it. She said that I always figure out a way to make something work, which was kind of nice to hear, but we still hadn't arrived at the true reason that I'd climbed up the pole. That didn't happen until Joe remarked, "You know, you didn't ask us for help at all."

Somewhat surprised, I said, "It didn't even occur to me." At that moment, I realized that I certainly encourage everyone else on the planet to ask for assistance, and I ask for it to a degree, except when I get to a place like the top of that pole—a feeling of complete powerlessness, helplessness, and loneliness. The next words that came out of my mouth originated from somewhere that I'd been unaware of consciously. I said, "When I get to a place like that, and this has been true throughout my life, it's impossible for me to turn my physical body over to anyone else's suggestion."

When I made that comment, I looked at Carin and felt an immediate sense of knowing between us. She understood exactly what I meant, and tears came to my eyes. We both knew at a very deep level that this dynamic had manifested itself in my life and in our relationship, and now it all made sense. For the first time, we both understood why I'd behaved as I had in certain situations.

You see, early in my life, I'd experience huge pain when anyone would suggest anything to me concerning my body or behavior. That's as much as I'll say about it, because the true genesis of this pain is too personal for me to share in this book. (If I were ever to meet you in a therapeutic situation and I deemed it appropriate, I would certainly share it with you.) But suffice it to say that all behavior is logical. There's a reason that I haven't been open to suggestions unless I requested them myself, and it's

As children,
we come up with
ingenious ways
to protect
ourselves,
but those
defense
mechanisms
later turn into
emotional prisons.

been an impediment to my closeness with all human beings throughout my entire life.

This is the case with a lot of people who are trauma survivors. As children, we come up with ingenious ways to protect ourselves, but those defense mechanisms later turn into emotional prisons. That had happened to me, and I suddenly became aware of the damage it had caused. All at once, I realized that the worst-case scenarios I'd imagined were just stories—they had nothing to do with reality, and they had nothing to do with my climbing that pole.

The universe, in its infinite wisdom, had just offered me an opportunity to discover something significant—it was time for me, once and for all, to take Step 4 and get the aid I needed to heal this very deep scar.

Finally Dissipating the Fear

As a result of what occurred at the Quantum Leap, Carin and I went to a session with my good friend Brent Baum (whose work I mentioned in *It's Not about the Horse*) a few days later. Brent is a trauma specialist and a gifted therapist, and we were hoping he could help us put these new observations that came to me after climbing the pole into perspective.

Brent was able to show me that what had occurred on top of the pole was nothing more than a reenactment of something that had been played out infrequently throughout my life. Due to the emotional wounds in my early life, I'd created an existence of polarization. Let me explain what this means.

Prior to about the age of nine and a half, I don't recall being a rage-filled kid. In fact, I remember being quite sensitive and frightened for the most part, with a general anxiety about living in the world. However, something occurred when I was nine and a half that set up a pattern for future behavior.

I was in my boyhood home in Georgia with my older brother and my grandmother, whom I loved dearly. My brother was teasing me, as siblings will do, but this instance must have been significant in some way, because I remember it in detail. I recall finding myself in overload emotionally, as if to say, "I can't take another minute of this!" As if I'd been put on automatic pilot, I ran into the kitchen and grabbed the biggest butcher knife we had. I went toward my brother with it and told him that if he didn't leave me alone, I would—and I remember saying this—cut his guts out. I remember him looking at me as if I'd lost my mind. He immediately stopped teasing me and walked away. When my grandmother told me to put the knife away, I threatened her as well. I was truly in a trancelike state. That behavior did not go unnoticed, and I was later punished—and rightly so. In a civilized society, it's not okay to pull a knife on your family.

That day, something clicked in my head and it's been with me ever since. My rage-filled behavior had come up in total response to the shame, fear, embarrassment, and pain of being teased by my brother. Rage seemed to stop those unwanted emotions when they came from an external source, and I later discovered that it also seemed to stop them when they came from inside as well. Whenever I felt those "weak" feelings, rage allowed me to shut myself off emotionally, look at the other person, and angrily think, *Fuck you! Who needs you?* Through the emotion of rage, I could separate from others and become totally unavailable.

As Brent questioned me about how this had manifested itself in my life, I realized for the first time that I'd been associating vulnerability with helplessness and hopelessness. Until that moment, I'd always believed that if I *was* helpless and hopeless, I'd be rejected. Emotionally, that's what vulnerability meant to me, even if intellectually, I know it's the furthest thing from the truth. Children, when they're vulnerable, are sometimes helpless; we grown-ups

131

But using rage as a weapon as an adult became a cell in my emotional prison.

are not—we've proven that simply by growing up. I'd just never known how to be vulnerable and a grown-up at the same time before.

As a little boy, pulling that knife had served as a temporary solution. But using rage as a weapon as an adult became a cell in my emotional prison. Whenever I felt threatened, the anger would leave me standing there, trapped with a figurative knife in my hand. Rage kept me kept me safe to some degree, because it prevented me from feeling shame, and it pushed people away when I perceived them as being dangerous. However, it also kept me from being close to people whom I wanted to love. I was desperately afraid that when I really cared for someone, it might translate into pain and rejection. Being caught between these two opposite extremes—rage at the one end, pain and rejection at the other—resulted in the polarization I mentioned earlier. Crazy? Yes. Logical? Absolutely.

Sitting there in Brent's office, I realized that the place I was looking for was the midpoint between those two poles. I didn't have a clear map, but I became committed to finding such a place, because I will not spend the rest of my time on this planet living in this way.

As Brent, Carin, and I continued our session, I also began talking about my perception of what was expected of me in our marriage. For as long as I can remember, I've had the notion that my job was to be strong, have answers, and be there for others, especially for any woman with whom I was in a relationship. I truly wanted to be completely open and intimate with Carin, yet such vulnerability equaled hopelessness, helplessness, and powerlessness in my mind. As I explored these feelings, I found myself feeling very small internally, and for maybe the fourth or fifth time in my life, I was able to go into a depth of sadness and pain that I've kept mostly at bay for my entire existence.

I began to talk about our dog, Toby, whose cancer has recurred. I've truly grown to love this dog, who comes up to our bed in the morning and lays his muzzle on my hand. In a small voice, I said, "I don't get to grieve; I don't get to feel disappointed; I don't get to feel the pain of the potential loss of a great friend like Toby, because I believe that I have to be there for Carin." This was a deep expression of love, but it came from the place of being a helpless young boy, not an empowered grown man. It turns out that it was also just another story I'd made up—it wasn't what Carin expected at all.

I came to realize that I was still operating with the coping skills of a nine-and-a-half-year-old child who'd been afraid to deal with this particular source of fear and self-doubt. The route to my awareness involved climbing to the top of that pole and putting myself in a dysfunctional, perceived helpless-hopeless situation. By going through the process, I finally realized that I'm neither when I'm vulnerable.

(What really amazes me is that if I'd seen this in a client, my intellectual side would have been able to work with that person and offer plenty of opportunities. Somehow, I hadn't been able to do that for myself. I remember an old saying I heard years ago, and I guess it must be true: "A physician who treats himself has a fool for a patient." Just because I've been able to work therapeutically with others doesn't mean that I didn't remain blind to some of my own unresolved stuff.)

By the time we concluded the session, I was able to release more pain than I ever would have believed was there. Most important, I'd had a particularly enlightening breakthrough about an experience that had occurred a year or so before. At that time, I nearly destroyed my marriage—I'm fortunate that it's still intact.

My wife had asked me a question about a relationship I'd had prior to meeting her, and I'd lied about it. I continued to lie about it, because deep down inside, I believed that if I told her the truth, she would leave me. My wife has proven to me repeatedly how she feels about me, but my misperceptions just wouldn't let me believe that she valued me enough to accept what I'd done. She could have come up to me every day and told me how much she valued me, cooked me every special meal I ever wanted, made love to me 18 times a day, and sent me plaques for my wall, and it still wouldn't have changed my beliefs. How I felt about myself caused me to behave in ways that caused my wife to doubt herself.

Carin's intuition is extremely well honed, and my refusal to tell her the truth created a scenario that made her feel crazy. You see, Carin was aware of this other person and had an intuitive sense that something had occurred between us, but I wouldn't own up to it. Carin didn't care what I'd done prior to meeting her, but the fact that I didn't seem to trust her enough to tell her the truth was deeply painful for her. I didn't consciously mean to hurt her, but I subconsciously sure as hell did, due to my own belief system about whether or not anyone would value me enough to stay with me. Once again my history, which had nothing to do with my wife, had gotten in the way of a relationship that I valued and treasured beyond words. In spite of my conscious valuing of that, I damn near trashed it.

One of the things that was very clear throughout this turbulent time was how my anger came into play. Every time Carin questioned me, I became indignant, which was in direct proportion to my being afraid that at any given moment she might find out that I'd lied. It was the same old pattern: feel

Once again my history, which had nothing to do with my wife, had gotten in the way of a relationship that I valued and treasured beyond words.

vulnerable, get scared, get embarrassed, get angry. I was in the exact same place that occurred when I was a foot and a half from the top of the pole at the Quantum Leap. I was frozen with fear, feeling help-less and hopeless, with no relief in sight, and I wouldn't ask for anyone's help. Once again, the same old story that I'd made up in my head was keeping me from dealing with the problem at hand.

Now, here's one of the most interesting things I learned from this whole experience. In trying to avoid my worst-case scenario, I made it happen anyway. I was sure that if I told Carin the truth, she'd leave me. I was afraid I'd never be close to her—but by lying to her and causing her to doubt her intu-ition and her very sanity, I drove her away anyway. Hell, she was gone emotionally, and our closeness was damaged by my lie. She knew better; I knew bet-ter. The elephant was in the room—I was unwilling to acknowledge just how big it was, how bad it stank, and that it was blocking my view.

As I said in the Preface, I've never gotten away with anything, and that certainly continues to be true. Eventually, when the truth was revealed by someone else, it almost cost me my marriage. The key word here is *almost:* Almost may be significant when it comes to horseshoes and hand grenades, but it's not worth much in a marriage. I came close to losing Carin, but I didn't. In fact, this whole experience ultimately brought us the closeness I'd always hoped for.

Naturally I don't recommend any of this as a way to create closeness in a marriage. The simplest thing would have been for me to confront my own demons and fears without involving my wife and dragging her through my mud. I nearly destroyed the thing I wanted most in order to come to that awareness, and I offer this example in hopes of helping others avoid such pain.

So, did I learn something? Yes, I think I gathered quite a bit of information and support in walking through Step 4.

1. First of all, this won't be happening again, because what Carin and I have gone through has brought us to new levels of intimacy—none of which has been very easy, by the way, and all of which was of my making. Nothing is worth going through this again. I'd never risk losing Carin and what we have together.

I wasn't just setting boundaries, I was absolutely drawing a line in the sand and saying, "If you come across this, somebody's going to end up being hurt— and it won't be me."

2. Second, if I ever climb up that pole again or if I ever get to that spot of helplessness and hopelessness, I'm going to start talking about it. And if anybody suggests something to me, I'm not going to cut them off. I realize that's what I've done my whole life, and it hasn't worked very well.

3. Finally, I now understand what caused me to set my boundaries with such a vengeance. I wasn't just setting boundaries, I was absolutely drawing a line in the sand and saying, "If you come across this, somebody's going to end up being hurt—and it won't be me." People get that message, and they back off from someone who says such things and appears a little bit crazy when you look in their eyes. That's what a really scared person will do, and that's what I'd done when I felt really helpless. I was using the coping skills of a terrified child, and they didn't get me what I wanted. Fortunately, I now have a new awareness.

At the end of our session, both Carin and Brent told me how much lighter my face looked and how unburdened I appeared to be. It certainly felt that way to me. It was such a relief to have taken this crucial fourth step. I'd gathered information, confronted some lifetime misperceptions, and finally walked through the fear that had held me back for so long. In allowing myself to be vulnerable to another human being, I'd discovered the sweetness of connection and the joy that is every individual's birthright. And that's when I knew that I was finally ready for the last step in this process, a step I'd never been able to fully realize before.

❖ ❖

Step 5

Celebrate!

Just as I'd suspected, taking the Quantum Leap to conquer my acrophobia was like peeling an onion. As I pulled back one layer of fear and self-doubt, additional layers were revealed—as were new opportunities to heal old wounds. Of course this doesn't mean that I've cleared up all my fears for the rest of my life. I just handled <u>one</u> specific kind in that particular moment.

I also have a fear of the ocean, which wasn't cured by this experience. If I want to overcome that, I'll have to get in the water and use the five steps, just like I did with my fear *of heights. In other words, it's kind of like aspirin, which is good for a lot of different ailments, but I'd use a different dosage for a headache than I would for arthritis or to prevent a heart attack. Now, the aspirin is the same drug in each of those three cases, but in different situations it produces different results. The steps operate under the same principle: They're five tools for one horrible thing (fear and self-doubt) that manifests itself in a lot of ways.*

We start out on a journey, working toward a specific destination—to climb a pole, get over a fear of the sea, or whatever the case may be—and if we are to awaken from the sleep of the physical life into the spiritual, then we have to understand that all of our hoped-for results turn out to be opportunities. All we have to do is be willing to take that first step and see where it leads, then take the opportunities that arise from that place. The end result is a celebration that makes the whole process worthwhile.

It's Time to Rejoice!

Once we've completed the first four steps, we arrive at a place of knowing that there's nothing wrong with us and there wasn't that much to be afraid of in the first place. So now it's time to consciously claim this place as our own. After all, we didn't get lucky—we've *earned* the right to kick up our heels because we've done what we didn't believe we could do. We've corrected a misperception that made us believe we were faulty and that the world was an unsafe place. All of a sudden, we know that's not true—we're not faulty and we are safe. So let's celebrate!

How long will we be able to stay in that festive place? Sometimes it may be as brief as five to ten seconds, but even that can be enough time to integrate the possibility of it happening again. The one thing I know about the human spirit is that if we prove something to it, it will reach for that thing time and time again. All we need is the willingness to confront the fear and self-doubt, which is where the first four steps of this process come in. Finally, these steps all lead to freedom, and that's ultimately what we're really looking for. After all, if there weren't results along the way, I wouldn't expect anyone (including myself) to continue on the journey.

One of the things that I'd like to share with you is what happened immediately following the deep emotional work that took place in Brent Baum's office. A few days after our session, Carin and I experienced a huge shift in the energy of our home. You see, as couples get closer to discovering their individual core wounds by clearing up the pain of the past, the energy often intensifies. Anyway, as I previously mentioned, before I climbed the pole I was extremely defensive at any given moment, and would go into a trauma-triggered place where I had absolutely no skills as a husband, a partner, or even a friend—I'd raise my voice, walk away, dissociate, or simply go cold inside. I'd developed all those skills over the years as a way to isolate myself and keep from experiencing the worst-case scenario, which was to die from whatever I was afraid of. Suddenly, all of that was gone. Since that day in Brent's office, I haven't felt anywhere near the amount of tension I'd experienced before. I finally stopped acting like some kind of tomcat with a gland condition, spraying the room to keep myself safe.

Progress is being made. I know that I'm heading toward the middle ground that I seek, and I've seen it happen to many others as well. In fact, one of the common misperceptions that I'm repeatedly confronted with, both in my practice and in my personal life, is that our particular fears and insecurities are unique to us. In other words, we convince ourselves that we're alone—we're sure that these kinds of things never, ever happen to anyone else. My good friend DB recently reminded me of just how much company I have on my particular journey.

DB's Story

DB heard about my experience at the Quantum Leap and told me that he wanted to come to Miraval and attempt the climb himself, since his acrophobia was similar to mine. It turns out that he had many fears and wounds that I could relate to.

Early in his life, my friend had lost both of his parents within a short time. His father died when DB was 11 years old, and three years later his mother passed away, too. The young boy and his brother were left in the care of relatives who were kind enough to raise them, but conditions were attached: After age 18, the brothers either had to go to school or they'd have to leave their relatives' home. They both elected to leave.

DB met, fell in love with, and married a woman who went on to become the mother of his only child, a developmentally challenged daughter. After a number of years together, the wife developed breast cancer and subsequently died. DB was at her side throughout the whole ordeal, hearing her scream in agony but unable to do anything but watch.

After his wife's death, DB was unable to experience any kind of lasting relationship. He generally chose unavailable women who were very different from him or who were unable to be in his life along with his daughter. During his stay at Miraval, we discovered that the reason DB had done this to himself is because he subconsciously believed that if he allowed himself to love someone, she'd leave him. (Sound familiar?)

I've said before that all behavior is logical. As we looked back at DB's life, it was easy to see why he'd developed a belief system that said, "Everyone I love always leaves." He blamed himself for the deaths of his father, mother, and wife, believing that if he'd done something different, they would have lived. He'd experienced these traumas as a child without having the tools to deal with them, and he hadn't allowed himself to go there since. Now 48 years of age, DB brought all this history with him as he attempted to make the Quantum Leap.

He'd asked me to facilitate the climb for him, and I was more than honored to be at his side. As Joe and Kevin prepped him, DB vocalized his fears both internally and aloud. He said, "I hate this. I *hate* this. I hate being afraid like this. I can't stand it. I don't want to do this, but I've got to." I asked him to quantify the fear, and he said it was about a nine or ten. He told me his worst-case scenario, which was that he'd get to a point where he wouldn't know what to do and would feel powerless and helpless, just as I had. He'd heard me talk about not asking for assistance and was committed to avoiding the same mistake.

DB had worked out in his head what needed to happen once he got to the top, yet when it finally happened, he was unprepared. As he stepped off the ladder and on to the staples, he found himself feeling agitated and frightened. When he was only two steps away from the top—at almost exactly the same point I'd frozen up—he stopped and remarked, "I'm stuck."

"Do you remember your worst-case scenario?" I called up to him.

He answered, "It's happened. I don't know what to do."

I suggested that he be still for a moment and determine what type of help he would need.

After a few seconds, he asked, "Is there another set of staples above my feet?"

"Yes," I replied, noticing that DB had intuitively gone from "I don't know what to do" to taking the next step. He placed first one foot and then the other on the next pair of staples, and his knees were level with the platform. He'd already gone farther than I

DB's Story

had in his journey. Then he asked for help: "Would you give me tension on the security rope and help steady me as I try to take the next step?"

I agreed, yet as DB tried to step out on the platform, he lost his balance and fell. The harness caught him, but he skinned his shin pretty badly as he stepped up. I asked if he needed help with that.

"No, it's not bad at all," he said. Then he added, "This is where I usually freeze—when I experience a little bit of pain, I get afraid and go no further. This is what I do in my life and in my relationships."

DB had come to his worst-case scenario, had known intuitively what to do, and decided to try something different from what he'd done for the past few decades. On his third attempt, he stood upright on the pole. As he gazed out at the view, I suggested that maybe he needed to release the souls of his mother, father, and wife into the Santa Catalina Mountains that he saw in the distance.

He shouted at the top of his lungs, "I set you all free to go live in the mountains or any other place you choose!" Then, launching himself off the pole toward the mountains, he yelled, "Freedom! Freedom!" as loudly as he could, and was caught in the harness for a safe descent.

After Joe and Kevin lowered DB to the ground and we sat down to talk about his climb, we all realized that DB had achieved at the top of the pole

what I later accomplished in reviewing my experience with Brent Baum and Carin. Using the five
steps to break through our fear and self-doubt,
we'd each taken a different route to get to the same
place of surrender and self-awareness.

I've spoken with DB several times since this
experience, and he told me an interesting story. He
was on the road, covering a convention, when a
woman walked past the booth where he was working. He turned to the co-worker beside him and said,
"That's the kind of woman I should be with."

"What was so remarkable about that?" I
wondered.

"Well, Wyatt, this wasn't the type of woman I'd
usually choose," he replied. "She looked like someone who had probably been through the fire like
myself, and I instantly felt that I might relate to and
feel safe with her."

So DB walked over, introduced himself, and
chatted with the woman for a few minutes. She then
produced a book that was very special to her from
her purse and said, "This was given to me, and it's
very important to me, yet I feel an immediate urge
to share it with you . . . so here you go."

DB was so touched by this gesture that in the
week after that encounter, he and his new friend
maintained communication via e-mail and telephone
(since she lives in Florida and he lives in California). He

added that the conversations with her have been some of the best he's ever had, and he's enjoying getting to know this woman on a safe, soul level. He really is celebrating life now, in the best way possible.

Endings . . . and Beginnings

As you can see, DB and I are two souls who have had similar experiences. Although we faced losses that manifested themselves differently, our spirits defended themselves similarly, and we both found a sense of release and freedom in the same Quantum Leap activity. I'm repeatedly reminded each time I take a step—or witness someone else taking their particular steps—that our journeys are both unique and similar in their nature. We're all about to "get it," and if we're willing to share our "getting it" with each other, the journey is certainly sweeter.

Today, I feel more free from fear and self-doubt than I ever have in my entire life. Will there be more fear and self-doubt, more challenges to conquer, more things to learn? Absolutely. As is the case with most of life's journeys, climbing that pole at the Quantum Leap was nothing more than a beginning.

I remember that in one of my favorite movies, *The Dark Crystal,* a character named Aughra is describing the conjunction of the planets that will

157

mark the end of the world. When the three suns are in conjunction, she explains, it will represent the end and also the beginning. "End, begin, all same," she says.

The same is true for us, I think. Most of my life, I've hoped for a solution, a definitive solution—but what I've found are beginnings, beginnings, and more beginnings. This experience was no different.

When I began writing this book, my intent was to climb up a 30-foot pole and document what happened as I faced my fear of heights. In the process, because I was open and willing to examine whatever came up, I discovered a whole family of interrelated insecurities, and by using the five steps, I was able to handle them one by one.

I didn't think I could get to the top of that pole; I didn't think I could become vulnerable in a relationship without being seen as helpless and hopeless; I didn't think I could be completely honest without being abandoned; and, for a short period of time, when I was completely at a loss for words, I didn't think I could write this book. Well, I not only wrote it, but by walking through the fear and self-doubt, I corrected a belief system—my own misperceptions—and came out celebrating on the other side. Will miracles never cease? (And in addition to all that, I get to keep the money!)

Afterword

The Sweetness of Connection

*A*s I've mentioned, deciding to grow spiritually can be a lonely journey. However, lately I seem to run into more and more individuals who are taking the same journey and walking through their own fear and self-doubt. So, as a final note, I'd like to tell you about one of the deepest, sweetest connections I've ever felt with my fellow human beings.

In April of 2002, I had the opportunity to spend three days in New York City, presenting a workshop for the staff of a national magazine. The day I arrived, documentary filmmaker and friend Barry Boyle greeted me at my hotel in Times Square, and we proceeded to go to Ground Zero, the former site of the World Trade Center.

The trip from Times Square to the neighborhood where the twin towers had once stood was an event in and of itself. It was my first trip on a subway, and I'd heard all kinds of terrible stories over the years about New York's subway system. None of them turned out to be true; in fact, beneath the streets of the city, I consistently connected with people.

I was wearing a big hat, and one lady tapped me on the shoulder and said, "You might want to hold on to the support bar. I'd hate to see you get that beautiful hat knocked off." I asked her what tipped her off that I wasn't a veteran of subway travel, and this gave several of us an opportunity to laugh with each other. Conversations continued to occur with people I'd never met in my life, and lots of folks smiled at me as I made my way toward the Ground Zero site. This had been my experience in New York on two previous occasions, so maybe we do get what we ask for—I was certainly being open to the people of the city, and they responded in a most favorable way.

What occurred at the end of that subway ride was one of the greatest experiences of my life, and I'll never forget it as long as I live. Barry and I came up out of the subway and took a cab to the cordoned-off viewing area that surrounded the site, and the first thing I noticed was how clean the area was. It was

162

nothing like the horrendous debris I'd seen on TV. Other than the absence of those huge towers and some construction around the area, there was no evidence that this catastrophic event had even occurred. I thought, *How incredible of people to come in and restore some semblance of order to an area that had been so completely devastated.*

The church that sits to the right of Ground Zero was spotless, while the fence around it was covered with what must have been hundreds of thousands of expressions of sympathy, love, and respect for those who had lost their lives. I remember thinking that approximately 3,000 people had lost their lives on 9/11, which in turn had somehow provided countless people an opportunity to connect as fellow participants on this journey on Earth.

As Barry and I walked toward the ramp that led to Ground Zero, I realized that even if I spent a week there, it would have been impossible for me to count all the cards, bouquets, ribbons, and plaques of acknowledgment directed toward the victims. God only knows how many heartfelt notes had been written—it seemed as if every country on the planet had been represented there by expressions of sympathy and support. I felt incredible sorrow as I reached up and touched the signatures on the plywood walls that lined the ramp. I walked to the edge of the barricade and looked into the empty

163

space that had housed those two magnificent build-ings and all those wonderful souls who were sim-ply living their lives on a daily basis. As Barry told me later, "I've never seen a sadder look on any-body's face than when you looked over the edge into where the towers were."

I remember thinking in the midst of my grief that I definitely felt a sense of connection to people all over the world, due to the massive outpouring from those who had done what they could to say, "I'm sorry this happened." I wish we could get the message that this opportunity to show what's in our hearts exists on a daily basis, and that we needn't wait for a tragedy as an excuse to express our feel-ings toward our fellow human beings.

All of those souls who died gave the rest of us an opportunity to open up our hearts. Does that make up for their loss? Of course not. But there seemed to be some spiritual justice involved with what I witnessed that day, more than half a year after the tragedy of 9/11 had occurred.

As Barry and I stood quietly looking at the emptiness of the space, a young man and his wife came up. He was about 6'8", but she was in a wheelchair and couldn't see over the four-and-a-half-foot barrier that kept people from entering the site. What occurred next brought tears to my eyes. This gentle giant bent all the way down to the ground, balancing himself on one leg and easing himself back between her legs. He placed her legs around his waist; she wrapped her arms around his neck; and this big, strong man stood up with her and walked to the edge of the barricades with her on his back so that she might see Ground Zero for herself.

When I talk about the opportunity to connect and the sweetness of that action, I recall that day in April 2002, and I will continue to remember it for the rest of my life. It shows what's possible when we let ourselves overcome our fears and insecurities and reach out to each other.

❖ ❖

Acknowledgments

*W*hen I thought about the people to whom I would express my gratitude for making this book possible, where I would start was certainly a no-brainer: I start with you, the readers. Without all of you who were kind enough to open up your checkbooks, your hearts, and your curiosity to an unknown writer, I wouldn't be writing this second book. So, to all of you who took the time to buy, read, and recommend *It's Not about the Horse*, I thank you from the bottom of my heart.

To Cheryl Richardson, I would not have had my initial book deal if not for your generosity, encouragement, and the kindness of your spirit. My association with you has been rich, rewarding, and filled with gratitude and laughter. In a million years, I couldn't begin to express with words how much I appreciate you. I thank you so much for introducing me to my publisher, Hay House; for taking time to encourage me; and for always having your phone lines open to me when I got stuck and didn't think I could do this. I truly appreciate your encouragement and mostly your friendship. It's been a joy working with you, and I look forward to many more days and nights of working in conjunction with you and the people who are kind enough to spend time with us in our workshops.

I am so deeply grateful for the staff at Hay House—I thank you all for being nothing but kind, supportive, and generous with me. Reid Tracy, you're one of a kind and I hope you know that—the people who know you are certainly aware of it. Thank you so much for believing in me and my work, and for giving me the opportunity to express myself to an audience this large. Danny Levin, thanks for your friendship, your support, your encouragement, your constructive criticism at times, your laughter, and your heart. You're a good man, and I appreciate you. Gail Fink, thank you so much for

your expertise and your particular gifts in helping to put this book together. I appreciate it.

To Sue Adkins, for the hours that you've spent walking through my Southern accent and transcribing all of this dictation, some of which I'm sure didn't make sense at times—thanks for your patience, your skills, and your willingness to go the extra mile with me. I'm glad you were part of this. You certainly made it much easier for me to do this work.

To Brent Baum, thanks for your friendship and your gifts of healing. I shall always treasure having known you. You've been a true gift in my life.

Dr. Gregory Koshkarian, I'm literally able to thank you from the bottom of my heart, due to your fixing it and helping it to heal. And to Dr. T. K. Warfield and Dr. Mary Klein—I hope you both know how special you've been in enriching the lives of my family.

I also wish to give tons of thanks to an organization called Miraval Life in Balance™. I'm very fortunate and blessed to be able to work at a place like Miraval, in one of the greatest spots on the planet, Tucson, Arizona. Thank you to everyone there, from the line staff to upper management. To my colleagues at the Purple Sage Ranch, thank you so much for your support and your friendship. Jack O'Donnell and Amy McDonald, thank you both for your encouragement and support.

I'd be remiss in not thanking the people who have been the most important in forming my career as a therapist—and that's *every client I ever worked with*. You were also my teachers in the process. Thank you so much for sharing your lives with me, for trusting me with your secrets, and for allowing me to relate, in a general way, the stories of your miracles with the rest of the world. They've been so important for people; in fact, you may never know how much each of you has contributed to the healing of the planet simply by doing your own healing. Let me assure you that you have. What you've done not only matters to you, it matters to others, and I thank you.

Finally, I'm grateful for the blessing of living in the United States of America, where I'm allowed the freedom of expressing myself in whatever manner I see fit, with the only fear of reprisal coming from the stories I make up.

About the Author

*W*yatt Webb, the author of *It's Not about the Horse* (with Cindy Pearlman), survived 15 years in the music industry as an entertainer, touring the country 30 weeks a year. Realizing he was practically killing himself due to drug and alcohol addictions, Wyatt sought help, which eventually led him to quit the entertainment industry. He began what is now a 22-year career as a therapist. A job at his original rehab center in Nashville, Tennessee, evolved into his becoming a successful workshop facilitator, lecturer, and author who approaches his work with passion and commitment.

Today, Wyatt is one of the most creative, uncon-
ventional, and sought-after therapists in the country. He's the founder and leader of the Equine Experience at Miraval Life in Balance™, one of the world's
premier resorts, which is located in Tucson.

If you'd like to learn more about Wyatt Webb's
Equine Experience programs held throughout the
year at Miraval, please call: (800) 232-3969.

Notes

Notes

Notes

Notes

Notes

Notes

Notes

Notes

Notes

Notes

We hope you enjoyed this Hay House book. If you would like to receive a free catalog featuring additional Hay House books and products, or if you would like information about the Hay Foundation, please contact:

Hay House, Inc.
P.O. Box 5100
Carlsbad, CA 92018-5100

(760) 431-7695 or (800) 654-5126
(760) 431-6948 (fax) or (800) 650-5115 (fax)
www.hayhouse.com

※ ❀ ※ ❀ ※

Published and distributed in Australia by:
Hay House Australia Pty. Ltd. • 18/36 Ralph St.
Alexandria NSW 2015 • *Phone:* 612-9669-4299
Fax: 612-9669-4144 • www.hayhouse.com.au

Published and distributed in the United Kingdom by:
Hay House UK, Ltd. • Unit 62, Canalot Studios
222 Kensal Rd., London W10 5BN
Phone: 44-20-8962-1230 • *Fax:* 44-20-8962-1239
www.hayhouse.co.uk

*Published and distributed in the Republic of South
Africa by:* Hay House SA (Pty), Ltd., P.O. Box 990,
Witkoppen 2068 • *Phone/Fax:* 2711-7012233
orders@psdprom.co.za

Distributed in Canada by:
Raincoast • 9050 Shaughnessy St.,
Vancouver, B.C. V6P 6E5
Phone: (604) 323-7100 • *Fax:* (604) 323-2600

※ ❀ ※ ❀ ※